Your Towns and Cities in the G.

Liverpool

in the Great War

Dedicated to the memory of the
Hillsborough 96

Your Towns and Cities in the Great War

Liverpool
in the Great War

Stephen McGreal

Pen & Sword
MILITARY

First published in Great Britain in 2014 by
PEN & SWORD MILITARY
an imprint of
Pen and Sword Books Ltd
47 Church Street
Barnsley
South Yorkshire S70 2AS

ISBN 978 1 47382 161 3

A CIP record for this book is available from the British Library

Printed and bound in England
by CPI Group (UK) Ltd, Croydon, CR0 4YY

Typeset in Times New Roman by Chic Graphics

Pen & Sword Books Ltd incorporates the imprints of
Pen & Sword Archaeology, Atlas, Aviation, Battleground, Discovery,
Family History, History, Maritime, Military, Naval, Politics, Railways,
Select, Social History, Transport, True Crime, and Claymore Press,
Frontline Books, Leo Cooper, Praetorian Press, Remember When,
Seaforth Publishing and Wharncliffe.

For a complete list of Pen and Sword titles please contact
Pen and Sword Books Limited
47 Church Street, Barnsley, South Yorkshire, S70 2AS, England
E-mail: enquiries@pen-and-sword.co.uk
Website: www.pen-and-sword.co.uk

Contents

Acknowledgements

To faithfully encompass the conditions prevailing upon the home front, the author has extensively consulted contemporary local newspapers. Any information relating to military activities had to be submitted to the Press Bureau prior to publication. And, much to the frustration of the author, Liverpool's war-time censors proved exceptionally diligent in their concealment of home-front activities. However, all was not lost for in the post-war years the *Liverpool Courier* published seventy-six special reports on Liverpool's part in the war. They have proved invaluable and allowed the snippets of information from the contemporary newspapers to be woven into this work. Having spent long days in Liverpool Reference Library trawling through micro film versions of contemporary newspapers, I wish to thank all the staff for their assistance. Roger Hull from the Archives Department for several images of munitionettes and the North Haymarket munition works. Mark Davies for the 'Flag Day' poster image, Peter Hart, Alan Wakefield, Vivien Healey and last but not least Ian Boumphrey, whose forebears managed the Cunard Munition Factory. Ian has generously provided treasured family Cunard Factory material for inclusion in this work and also other images for which I am very grateful.

Picture Credits

Introduction

In 1914, Britain was ill prepared for a modern mechanised conflagration, having prioritised its defence budget on developing the world's greatest navy at the expense of its small professional army. In direct contrast Germany had a slightly smaller fleet and the most powerful army in the world. Consequently, in the summer of 1914 as Britain took faltering steps along the path to Armageddon we were incapable of sustaining a protracted Continental war. Lord Kitchener famously appealed for a New Army of volunteers and recruiting officers were inundated with erstwhile recruits.

When Europe plunged into war an unprecedented arms race ensued and the civilian population strove to deliver the equipment and manpower so desperately needed in the front line. The citizens of Merseyside were no exception, for every personal and material force which constituted twentieth-century Liverpool was hurtled into the fight to preserve the British Empire. Geographically the port's location determined it became one of the major home bases of wartime operations. An estimated 150,000 men from Liverpool and district served in the First World War, and some 13,500 were casualties. The fighting qualities of Liverpool battalions are fairly well documented, but scant recognition has been made to those who provided the weapons and munitions. On the home front every normal civilian activity became a means of fund raising, each day was equivalent to Red Nose Day, Children In Need Day and every other worthy cause rolled into one. The First World War was greatly financed by people, who asked for and received nothing whatsoever from the state, but were still inspired by patriotism and allegiance to the king and the belief in their cause. Their trials and tribulations have mainly fallen into obscurity; arguably without the industrial powerhouse of the port and city of Liverpool, the victory we take for granted would not have materialised.

CHAPTER 1

A Summary of Nineteenth-century Liverpool

In 1207, on the eastern side of the Mersey estuary, a cluster of buildings fringing a sheltered creek and connecting tidal pool were granted a Royal Charter by King John. This elevation to market town status attracted tradesman and more inhabitants. Over the centuries mercantile trade gradually increased, and the first recorded American cargo arrived in 1648. But the harbour facilities were woefully inadequate so the increasing prosperous port employed Thomas Steers to design the world's first enclosed dock fitted with a watertight gate to eliminate tidal water rise and fall. The new dock opened in 1715, and four more docks followed.

In the latter part of the eighteenth century, Liverpool became a slaving port. Most of the town's principal merchants were involved in the 'Triangular Trade'. On the outward voyage Liverpool ships carried inexpensive goods which were exchanged for slaves, gold or ivory. On the 'middle passage', slaves were transported to America or the West Indies where they were sold. On the final leg of the triangle, Liverpool ships returned laden with cotton, sugar, rum and tobacco. The shameful trade became the backbone of Liverpool's prosperity. Some Liverpool slaves became free men, their legacy being Britain's oldest black community dating to a least the 1730s. The slave trade was officially abolished in 1807.

By 1801, Liverpool had a population of 77,000, and a decade later due to an abundance of employment the number had soared to 118,000.

A part of the Albert Dock today.

During the early nineteenth century, 40 per cent of the world's trade passed through Liverpool docks. To accommodate the burgeoning trade, in rapid succession robust new docks opened – Canning 1828, Clarence 1830, Brunswick 1832, Waterloo 1834, Trafalgar 1836, Canning 1842 and Albert Dock in 1846.

Across the river at the tidal inlet known as the Wallasey Pool, the first docks opened in 1847. Liverpool Corporation bought out their Cheshire competitor in 1855 and two years later a Royal Commission brought about the formation of the Mersey Dock and Harbour Board, tasked with controlling property and the collection of harbour dues.

Meanwhile, Liverpool elders demonstrated their civic pride and wealth by commissioning a succession of fine municipal buildings. The railway terminus at Edge Hill was extended into the heart of the city, Lime Street station opened in 1836. Five years later construction began on the neoclassical style St George's Hall, which opened in 1854.

Despite the town's wealth, for many it was a life of grinding poverty. The situation deteriorated during the 1840s, when hundreds of thousands of penniless Irish families fled the Great Famine and settled in Liverpool. By 1851, Liverpool had a population of 376,000, and of these approximately one-quarter were Irish-born. Liverpool's cosmopolitan communities broadened after 1865 due to Alfred Holt founding the Blue Funnel Line. His 'China Company' not surprisingly made regular sailings to China and the Far East. Former Chinese seamen settled in Liverpool founding the oldest Chinese community in Europe. The port continued to attract immigrants of diverse ethnicity, their traditions, customs and places of worship benefitting the culture of 'the world in one city'.

Some of the entrepreneurs had amassed considerable wealth including the American born cotton broker William Brown. He financed the William Brown Library and Museum, which first opened to the public in 1860. Andrew Barclay Walker, the brewery magnate, funded the construction of the first British public art gallery, the Walker Art Gallery, and it opened in September 1877. And, three years later, Queen Victoria granted Liverpool city status.

Another world first was the 1886 construction of a railway tunnel beneath a river. Above the Mersey, the dock system was almost

St George's Hall and Plateau.

completed, but severe dock traffic congestion impeded the efficient movement of goods and passengers. The solution was a pioneering 6½-mile-long overhead railway mainly operating 16ft (4.9m) above the roadway.

The world's first electric railway in the sky opened in 1893. Affectionately known as the Dockers' Umbrella, it remained in operation until 1956. In 1895 the Mersey Docks and Harbour Board opened the Riverside station terminus, which was adjacent to the Princess Landing Stage and conveniently sited for the transatlantic liners. The Lancashire and Yorkshire Railway Company (LYRC) trains using this station travelled slowly along tram-style tracks inset into the dock estate road surface before connecting with the London North West Railway main line network.

By 1906, the number of vessels using Liverpool numbered 6,357 and at about this time the familiar waterfront skyline began to emerge. At Stanley Dock some 27 million bricks formed the world's largest warehouse. The imposing bulk of the utilitarian design tobacco warehouse would be eclipsed by the elegant riverside buildings known as 'The Three Graces'.

The southern section of the filled-in George's Dock became the site of the Edwardian baroque-style Port of Liverpool building. Completed in 1907, it is better known as the Dock Offices. Adjacent to this stands the Royal Liver Assurance building, opened in 1911. This was the first major structure in the country made from reinforced concrete; the Liver bird surmounted domes have clock faces larger than Big Ben. The 18ft-high iconic Liver birds were sculpted by German born Carl Bernard Bartels (1866–1955), and despite being a naturalised Briton, his name would shortly be airbrushed from Liverpool history.

Three years later, work commenced on the third landmark, the Cunard Shipping Company headquarters. The architecture employed is a combination of Italian Renaissance and Greek revival; the company took possession in June 1916.

An abundance of unskilled workers drove wages downwards and throughout the nation workers demanded increased pay, improved working conditions and trade-union recognition. A seamen's dispute at Southampton Docks spread to other ports including Liverpool, where, in August 1911, an estimated 250,000 striking transport workers ensured nothing moved in or out of the city. Armed troops, police from

St Nicholas' Church and the overhead railway.

Riverside station was sandwiched between the river and Princes Dock.

ROYAL LIVER FRIENDLY SOCIETY HEAD OFFICES PIER HEAD LIVERPOOL	
LENGTH OF BUILDING	301 feet
WIDTH OF BUILDING	177 feet
HEIGHT, GROUND TO TOP OF LIVER BIRDS	322 feet
HEIGHT OF BIRDS	18 feet
NUMBER OF FLOORS (INCLUDING SIX IN EACH TOWER)	17
NUMBER OF LIFTS	17
NUMBER OF STEPS (BASEMENT TO TOWER)	483
THE LARGEST ELECTRIC TURRET CLOCK IN ENGLAND	
DIAMETER OF DIALS (2½ feet wider than those of "Big Ben")	25 feet
WEIGHT OF CLOCK MECHANISM	4 tons
WEIGHT OF FOUR PAIRS OF HANDS (WITH BEARING SPINDLES)	2 tons

The Liver Building.

The Liver Building and Dock Offices.

other forces and HMS *Antrim* standing by mid-river increased the tension which culminated in three days of rioting. During an attempt to liberate strikers from prison vans, two men were shot and killed by mounted soldiers. The acrimonious strike ended on 24 August after government intervention.

The Bootle coat of arms.

The following year the Gladstone Graving Dock (dry dock) was completed. This was the biggest in Europe and capable of accommodating the largest transatlantic steamers. The war interrupted the construction of the accompanying 3 miles (5km) of quays and warehouses, which finally became operational in 1927.

Approximately 4 miles north of Liverpool city centre stands the neighbouring borough of Bootle; the name reputedly derives from the Anglo Saxon Bold or Botle meaning a dwelling. In ancient times, on the sand hill-lined Mersey shore, a small hamlet developed around the Bootle spring. By the early nineteenth century Bootle had become a popular bathing resort for prosperous Liverpool citizens. However, the tranquillity ended during the 1840s when the arrival of the railways and the development of the Mersey docks transformed Bootle into a hive of industry. The population soared due to an abundance of employment and Irish immigration. The town's prosperity led to its elevation to a municipal borough in 1868 and in 1889 county borough status was granted.

Entwined in the history of Liverpool are the members of the King's Liverpool Regiment (KLR) whose ancestry dates from 1685, but the familiar title was only adopted in 1881. Harsh lessons experienced during the fairly recent South African war resulted in the re-organisation of the British Army in 1908. With regards to the King's Liverpool Regiment, the re-shuffle led to two regular infantry battalions serving alternatively at home or overseas. The regiment had two Special Reserve Battalions, and the Volunteer battalions, and after the 1908 reforms the latter became components of the Territorial Force. These Liverpool part-time soldier battalions were the 5th, the 6th (Rifles), the 7th, the 8th (Irish), the 9th and the 10th (Scottish). The Territorial Force existed purely for home defence, although individuals could elect for Imperial Service overseas. The six Liverpool Territorial battalions

1/7 King's Liverpool Territorials wearing the Imperial Service badge.

were organised and equipped by the West Lancashire Territorial Association, presided over by Lord Derby.

The association were also responsible for Liverpool's Territorial Artillery Corps. The 1st West Lancashire Brigade comprised three batteries. In late July 1914 they were stationed at Larkhill, Salisbury Plain where they were joined on 3 August by the Fourth West Lancashire (Howitzer) Brigade. The city also had the two batteries and ammunition columns of the Lancashire Heavy Brigade, Royal Garrison Artillery.

The Mersey Defences body were responsible for the defence of the port and the coastline extending from Formby to the Deeside village of Parkgate. The two principal corps involved were the Lancashire and Cheshire Royal Garrison Artillery (RGA) which manned the Mersey forts at Crosby, Perch Rock New Brighton and Seaforth. The Lancashire (Fortress) Engineers, Royal Army Medical Corps (RAMC), Army Service Corps (ASC) and others completed the city's defence.

To most citizens it would have been incomprehensible to consider that the assassination of the Archduke Franz Ferdinand and his wife in Sarajevo on 28 June 1914 would precipitate a chain of events culminating in the outbreak of the First World War. The fundamental causes paving the road to war were nationalistic ambitions, insecurity, expansion of territory and foolhardy military brinkmanship.

Seeking reparations for the assassinations by Bosnian-Serb assassins, Austria-Hungary, prompted by Germany, made a series of uncompromising demands on Serbia. Most of these were met barring the issue of sovereignty. The British proposed a conference to arbitrate the issues; this was declined by Austria-Hungary, and on 28 July war was declared on Serbia. The European powers were obliged to honour treaties of support and the next day Russia commenced mobilising troops to intervene on behalf of their Serbian ally. Russia refused German demands to demobilise troops, and this led to the declaration of war on 1 August; two days later Germany declared war on France.

In readiness for war, the Germans had developed the Schlieffen Plan, which demanded a rapid advance in a great sweeping arc through France. The manoeuvre aimed to seize Paris and force the humiliated French to capitulate. Germany could then deal with the slowly mobilising Russian Army having avoided an unsustainable war on two fronts. But the German plan required free passage of its troops through neutral Belgium.

On 3 August 1914, plucky Belgium refused German demands of egress across their border; nonetheless, the following day Belgium was violated. It was a calculated gamble, for Germany doubted Britain would honour 'a scrap of paper', guaranteeing the protection of neutral Belgium. But, on 4 August Britain declared war on Germany, a war that many had thought probable, commencing at 11pm (midnight German time).

CHAPTER 2

1914
Eager for a Fight

As the storm clouds of war gathered, late July witnessed $12,000,000 of American gold being shipped to Europe. Britain, anticipating the imminent collapse of sterling and the international stock markets, imported $11,000,000 of gold. The suspension of the Stock Exchange followed and Liverpool businesses were under increasing pressure as apprehension grew concerning a European war. More noticeable precautionary measures involved the movement of troops and guarding of the rail network.

The Admiralty had long subsidised passenger liners on condition they would become auxiliary warships in war time. The debt was called in on 2 August when some of the finest and fastest liners were requisitioned for conversion to armed merchant cruisers. The Cunard Steam Ship Company berthed the giant *Aquitania* in Gladstone Dock, where over 6 days and nights almost 4,000 workers removed from the floating palace all non-essential furniture and fittings. After being stripped down to the bare ironwork and machinery, decks were stiffened, eight 6in guns, shell magazines, hoists and range finders were installed along with all the paraphernalia associated with a warship. On Saturday, 8 August, the *Aquitania*, predominantly manned by her peacetime officers and crew, left the Mersey. The vessel was the first of seventeen vessels converted on Merseyside for Liverpool's naval squadron of twenty-five armed merchant cruisers and a number of armed trawlers. Officially designated the 10th Cruiser Squadron, they operated in the water between the Shetlands and the Norwegian coast and between Iceland and the Arctic ice fields maintaining the distant Admiralty blockade of Germany. The *Aquitania* also served as a hospital and troopship.

On terra firma the threat of war dampened the 3 August Bank Holiday atmosphere. The *Evening Express* reported: 'The people went about their pleasures with a restraint that was altogether contradictory of the holiday spirit and entirely due to the ominous and imminent possibility of this country being plunged into war'.

Many prospective holidaymakers discovered that the London and North Western Railway Company (LNWR) had cancelled all excursions as well as a number of ordinary trains. Others braved the unsettled weather and took the boat to the seaside town of New Brighton, although the numbers at all the Cheshire resorts were down on previous years. Near Ellesmere Port, Hooton Park racecourse offered six races to punters, and further afield Lord Derby's horse 'Topic' won the 2pm Ovingdean Plate at Brighton. The Empire Theatre offered twice-nightly performances of the London sensational musical comedy *Dora's Doze* (possibly the origins of the derogatory term 'Dozy Dora'). The Rotunda Theatre offered twice-nightly performances of *The Madman* and pictures on the Rotunda Bioscope. The Royal Hippodrome advertised the imitable comedian Jimmy Learmouth as Colonel Cobb of the Red Hussars, supported by a full company of thirty artistes.

But there were other animated scenes in Liverpool's Lime Street, where large crowds congregated to greet the Territorials, who had been hastily recalled from distant annual training camps, or bid farewell to large numbers of naval reservists. The 4 August edition of the *Liverpool Daily Post and Mercury* reported: 'Wives and children, with tears streaming down their faces clung to husbands and fathers in passionate farewell. Young girls flung themselves into the arms of sweethearts whom, in their over-wrought state of mind, they imagined would never see again. The horror of approaching war had already laid its cold grip on their hearts.'

As the Liverpool Territorials poured into the city there was much activity in Seaforth Barracks, the Depot of the King's Liverpool Regiment. On mobilisation, the 1/King's where at Aldershot and after a roll call confirmed they were below war strength, reinforcements were despatched from the Depot. Once again Lime Street station was the scene of emotional farewells. The 1/King's Battalion was part of the 2nd Division of I Corps, commanded by Lieutenant General Sir Douglas Haig, itself a component of the British Expeditionary Force (BEF). On 12 August the King's and the 2nd South Stafford arrived at Southampton Docks where they boarded the SS *Irrawaddy* for France where the BEF would concentrate prior to engaging German forces. The 2/King's were stationed at Peshawar when war broke out and remained in India for the duration of the war.

Following mobilisation, the home-defence territorial battalions began locating to sites where they could be fully equipped, brought up to strength and undergo intensive training. The Liverpool Brigade would congregate at Knowsley Park.

The 5/King's assembled on 9 August in St George's Hall where Colonel McMaster requested their consent to offer the battalion for overseas service. The men unanimously agreed and the War Office was duly notified. The St Anne Street-based battalion then moved to Knowsley until 1 September prior to moving to Kent.

The 6/King's (Rifle) Battalion was assigned to the Mersey Defences and guarded the coast between Woodside and Hilbre Island until 9 August, when they were relieved by the 3/Cheshires. After returning to their Princess Park Barracks, the 6/King's trained at Sefton Park until 19 August when they moved to Knowsley. By the end of the month they had relocated to Croxteth Park, and a few days later they entrained to Kent. The battalion spent six weeks guarding the railway line extending from London to Newhaven, and by autumn they were camped at Canterbury.

The Bootle-raised 7/King's had their headquarters at 99 Park Street and were briefly billeted in the local schools prior to moving to Knowsley. Afterwards they spent several weeks guarding the railway track connecting Salisbury Plain and Southampton before relocating to Kent.

The 8/King's (Irish) battalion was based at 75 Shaw Street. Immediately on mobilisation they were assigned to Mersey Defences and established their headquarters at the Coronation Hall, Crosby. For ten days their duties involved guarding the power station of the Lancashire and Yorkshire Railway from saboteurs and manning coastal outposts as far as Formby. After being relieved by the 3/King's

The Liverpool Scottish, Edinburgh, 1914.

(Reserve) Battalion, they spent a fortnight billeted at St Francis Xavier's College, Shaw Street, until on 2 September they left for Knowsley.

The 9/King's headquarters was at 57 Everton Road. The battalion left the city for Dunfermline where on 13 August they became a component of the Firth of Forth defences.

The 10/King's (Scottish) Battalion hastily returned to their Fraser Street headquarters and prepared for war. On 7 August, 600 men were billeted at the Shakespeare Theatre, but due to overcrowding the boxing stadium in Pudsey Street was also utilised. This 'cuffs and collar' battalion also volunteered for overseas service. On 13 August their troop train departed Exchange station destined for Edinburgh where the battalion reinforced the Firth of Forth defences. On 10 October, the Liverpool Scottish went to Tunbridge Wells, Kent. On 1 November, the battalion sailed for France.

On 5 August the Lancashire (Fortress) Engineers took up their war stations. The Number 1 (Electric Light) Company was employed on Mersey Defences. Number 2 (Electric Light) Company departed for Ireland to assist in the Lough Swilly and Queenstown defences. Number 3 (Works) Company proceeded to Crosby where they worked alongside civilian labour and regiments training nearby creating coastal

RAMC Territorials at Calderstones Park, Liverpool.

earthworks and trenches for the defence of Liverpool. The defences were completed in December and Number 3 Company then left for Malta.

The 2nd West Lancashire Field Ambulance RAMC spent the first week of the war at headquarters amassing equipment and bringing the corps to full strength. The Territorials then relocated to Calderstones Park where they underwent rigorous training; they left their encampment in late October and proceeded to Kent. The Third Company had its headquarters at St Helens. After volunteering for overseas service, the Territorials proceeded to Knowsley Park for training until the end of October when they departed for Tunbridge Wells.

The West Lancashire Divisional Engineers also had their roots in St Helens, but men were also raised from other towns. On mobilisation, the 1st Field Company split into two work companies – one joined the Barrow Defence Force, the other went to Bidston (on the fringe of Birkenhead) where the territorial unit excavated trenches, erected road barriers and sentry posts; the 2nd Company went to Knowsley.

The local administration and distribution of the Territorials uniform and equipment was the responsibility of the Territorial Association which set up a Quartermasters Department in the drill halls of the West Lancashire RAMC and ASC at Tramway Road, Aigburth.

This synopsis of battalions does not profess to be a definitive listing of early war Liverpool-based units, for there are anomalies including the 3 (Reserve) Prince of Wales Volunteers (South Lancashire) Regiment which was based at Crosby from August 1914 until March 1917 and the Litherland-based 3/Royal Welsh Fusiliers. In the main, the Territorial battalions would eventually leave Merseyside, and the military vacuum would soon be filled by a new citizen army.

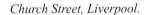

A commemorative £1 badge.

Far removed from the frenetic martial activity were the bankers who viewed with great apprehension an unprecedented run on the banks and Stock Exchange. The banking institutions closed until Friday, and during the respite the government took fiscal action including the printing and the first issue of £1 and later 10*s* notes, which were equivalent in value to the gold full and half sovereigns. The banks gradually withdrew sovereigns from circulation, a measure that aided gold reserves. Some £3,000,000 in £1 notes was available when the banks re-opened, and this form of quantitative easing temporarily continued at the rate of £5,000,000 a day.

The general public were indifferent to the financial crisis, and

Church Street, Liverpool.

Liverpool stores were crammed with customers panic buying provisions despite the drastic price increases. The various departments of Coopers' store in Church Street were so full the shop closed its doors, admitting only one customer at a time. Panic buying was replicated throughout the city, and at Leigh's in Byrom Street, where sugar was on sale at only 2*d* a pound (9*d* in Coopers), the store was besieged. Lord Mayor Herbert R. Rathbone appealed to the public for patriotic conduct by not buying provisions in excessive quantities, and this had the required effect. Within days the government introduced food price regulations and the Board of Agriculture announced there was five months' supply of breadstuffs in addition to the wheat and flour on sea passage.

Also under siege was the recruiting office headquarters in the Old Haymarket. Captain Finch, the recruiting officer for Liverpool, remarked: 'Recruits were being enrolled in such numbers that the staff were kept working at exceptionally high pressure dealing with the men. Many have had previous training either in the Regulars or Territorial's, but there are a large number of others who have not hitherto had any military training'.

From the four Poor Unions of Liverpool District, West Derby, the Parish of Liverpool, Toxteth and Birkenhead, their workhouses produced 300 men for the colours. The West Derby Union, the largest Poor Law authority in the country and comprising twenty-two parishes surrounding the city of Liverpool, probably furnished more men than any other single union. At Belmont Road workhouse the superintendent assembled suitable men and gave them a 'polite talk on patriotism', after which thirty to forty ex-army or navy men allegedly freely volunteered. On the arrival of a recruiting sergeant a further fifty enlisted at the Old Haymarket. The Brownlow Hill workhouse produced sixty recruits without counting reservists.

Mechanical or equine transport was also in demand. War Office agents were actively engaged requisitioning horses and commercial motor vehicles for military purposes; these were usually purchased outright for a fair price. Liverpool Corporation made a substantial contribution, as did large firms and small tradesmen such as milk dealers.

The government was also quick to implement defensive measures, and on the outbreak of war the nation began to metamorphose into a military garrison. The Board of Admiralty issued an order prohibiting the use of wireless telegraphy by merchant vessels in United Kingdom territorial waters. The nation's significant docks and quays became defended ports, with regulations appertaining to the Mersey stating: 'Boats have to pass through the examination anchorage and be examined by the examining officer. No vessel must be navigated or be at anchor between sunrise and sunset seaward of the line joining the Seaforth battery and New Brighton pier except she be entering or leaving port.'

The Lancashire and Cheshire RGA were responsible for the artillery defence of the Mersey. On 1 August, they were scheduled to leave for training at Shoeburyness but the order was rescinded. On 6 August, according to the *Liverpool Daily Post and Mercury*, a large Norwegian sailing vessel failed to comply with the signal from the Seaforth battery and continued on its course. A gun was then fired, but the warning had no effect. The Fort Perch Rock battery at New Brighton then fired one of its 6in guns, sending a shot across the ship's bows, which was followed by the immediate dropping of the anchor. The captain was ignorant of the fact Britain was at war. Later in the day the Allan liner *Mongolian* shared a similar experience when coming up the Mersey

The battery, New Brighton.

channel, but this time a gun shot went through her bows, but no casualties were reported.

At the beginning of August, Dr Utting, the chairman of the Port and Sanitary Committee (later Lord Mayor), granted the military authorities permission to use the infectious diseases hospital at Fazakerley. On 5 August, the hospital was formally handed over to the West Lancashire Territorial Association. A small RAMC Territorial unit, the 1st Western General Hospital had existed in Liverpool since 1908 and had arrangements in place for rapid expansion if necessary. The war strength would be achieved by the inclusion of 32 Liverpool 'a la suite' officers drawn from local medical specialists, 45 male Voluntary Aid Detachment (VAD) members and over 120 female nursing staff.

Three days later, the officer commanding, Lieutenant Colonel Burns Gemmel RAMC, a well-known Sefton Park practitioner, marched the corps into Fazakerley. The 1st Western General Hospital initially occupied the annexe until the main building was thoroughly disinfected and as each pavilion style ward became available it was prepared for military patients; the first sick military patient arrived on 11 August.

Following the creation of the Territorial Force, the West Lancashire Voluntary Aid Detachment came into existence with the intention of

1st Western General Hospital, Fazakerley.

raising male and female detachments to be trained in the transportation and care of the wounded during times of war. The pre-war organisation was governed by a committee including the prominent Liverpool physician Sir James Barr, who acted as County Director until mobilisation when the units came under his command. During the war there were no fewer than nineteen male and forty-four female detachments in West Lancashire connected with no fewer than forty-nine military hospitals.

The L&YRC Liverpool District Ambulance men were fully trained members of the St John Ambulance Association, as soon as war was declared the military authorities were offered and accepted the railway employees' services, designating them Number 7 VAD.

The Bootle Nursing Division of St John's Ambulance Brigade was formed in 1910, eventually becoming Female VAD Number 14. At a meeting in Bootle Town Hall on 12 August, Sir James Barr urged the women to assist in bringing the equipment up to war standard. They did so by collecting funds and making garments and bedclothes and appealing for the loan of a potential convalescent home.

The all-male Liverpool Ambulance Company, established in 1902, now offered their services to the military, the unit became VAD Number 25.

Another pre-war organisation, the Liverpool Civic Service League, had a voluntary body of men supplying an ambulance service within the city. After completing courses in first aid and ambulance work, their services were accepted by the West Lancashire Territorial Force Association, who designated them VAD Number 27.

Formed in January 1914, VAD Number 40 had at the commencement of hostilities twenty-six members with first-aid certificates. In common with other detachments, nursing lectures became a regular feature and volunteers increased rapidly.

Also in January 1914, as the result of a public meeting held at St Helens, a very large branch of the St John's Ambulance Brigade was created. On the outbreak of war this separated into two VAD detachments. Number 42 (Huyton) was commandeered by Mrs Bishop. The wife of Colonel Jackson RAMC and Assistant Director of Medical Services served as commandant of 44 VAD (St Helens) throughout the war.

In August 1914 Liverpool University also raised a detachment of students and lecturers who benefitted from eight courses of medical lectures in first aid and nursing. As September drew to a close twenty-five members passed St John examinations in nursing, and forty in first aid. The unit was officially recognised by the War Office in December and designated VAD 46.

A central bureau worked in conjunction with the Nursing Committee of the West Lancashire Division and VAD detachments. They had premises at 1 Gambier Terrace by the Anglican cathedral and existed for alleviating the needs of the military patients and for provision of comforts for those at the front. On 6 August, the Lady Mayoress, Winifred Rathbone, appealed to women of all classes to help in the care of the sick and wounded and the response was overwhelming. Appeals were also made for donations of hospital requisites, beds, bedding, pyjamas, clothing and cash. The bureau also

No. 1 Gambier Terrace is directly behind the car.

housed a cutting room, sewing room, bandaging room and offered ambulance classes throughout the war, and hundreds of thousands of items were produced.

In response to the appeal the Ladies Sefton Park West Conservatives Club, Aigburth Road opened a work depot for cutting out and making garments. A week later other branches operated at Mossley Hill Institute, St Agnes's Parish Room, Ullet Road, the Congregational Hall, Blundellsands and branches soon followed at Huyton, Gateacre and Allerton. In these genteel workshops most of the women received their first experience of industry.

However the biggest life-changing factor was sanctioned on 8 August when the House of Commons passed in five minutes emergency wartime regulations designed to stifle any undermining of the war effort. The Defence of the Realm Act (DORA) granted the government powers to suppress published criticism, imprison without trial and to commandeer resources, including buildings or land, required for the war effort; the act was regularly supplemented throughout the war.

Readers of the *Liverpool Evening Express* were also reminded of the Official Secrets Act 1911, under which:

any person is guilty of felony who, for any purpose prejudicial to the safety or interest of the State, approaches or enters a 'prohibited space', makes any sketch, plan, model or note which might be useful to an enemy; obtains or communicates any such sketch to another person; knowingly harbours anyone who he knows to have committed or be about to commit an offence under the Act, or permits such persons to assemble on his premises, or, having done so, refuses to disclose any information he may possess to a superintendent of the police. A 'prohibited place' under the Act includes any government work of defence, arsenal, factory, dockyard, ship, telegraph, or signal station, or place used for building, repairing, or storing ships, arms, or materials of war, or documents relating thereto.

As Liverpool was the next most important commercial centre to London, all persons were requested to be vigilant regarding the movements of strangers – especially foreigners, near any of the above sites. The authorities were to be alerted if anyone attempted to collect information on the movements and dispositions of troops. It was feared that spies might supply military information to the enemy to facilitate invasion, provide targets for hostile airships or sabotage the water supply or lines of communication, especially the railways.

An orchestrated wave of xenophobia swept the country; non-British citizens were now treated with suspicion in case they were enemy sympathisers. Residents were encouraged to assist the police and military authorities by reporting any suspicious movements of foreigners to the police. As a prelude of things to come, at the beginning of September a German pork butcher's shop in Stanley Road was attacked and looted.

After the introduction of a national Restriction Order any 'Alien Enemy', meaning any person of German or Austrian-Hungarian nationality, or subjects of any other state that might later be at war with the country, were required to register at the central police station if living temporarily or permanently in Liverpool. Aliens required a police permit to live in the defended port and could not travel more than 5 miles from their residence without police permission. Permits were also required for possession of a motor car, motorcycle or aircraft. They were further prohibited from possessing firearms, ammunition or explosives, or more than 3 gallons of flammable liquid, any signalling apparatus, carrier or homing pigeons and any cipher books or other means of secret correspondence.

Policing the regulations increased the pressure on the constabulary at a time when army reservists within the force were being mobilised. To make up the depleting numbers, part-time special constables were proposed. The Liverpool Civic Service League was formed during the 1911 strike and was somewhat resented due to the actions of its early members. For three years its services were not required, but the founder and chairman, Alderman Leslie, maintained an up-to-date roll of members. Following the declaration of war, Liverpool Civic Service League committee members agreed to dedicate their organisation to the various forms of war service. By 10 August, their secretary, Robert Gladstone Junior, was able to advise the first enrolment of males aged between 35 and 50 years old (who were not admissible as army recruits) would take place on 17 August. A donation of £50 financed sufficient drill instructors for the first 500 men. The corporation granted the use of the North Haymarket in Cazeneau Street where drills took place most evenings excluding Friday and Sunday. Within a few days the male section had a roll of 1,500 volunteers for special constable street duty, while others joined the Order of St John Ambulance Brigade and other agencies.

Meanwhile, on 7 August the vanguard of the 100,000-strong BEF arrived in France. After a few weeks' concentration, the British II Corps advanced to the southeast corner of Belgium, congregating around the town of Mons, where the Germans delivered a terrific onslaught. Hopelessly outnumbered, the BEF survivors retired, fighting rearguard actions as they withdrew towards the River Marne.

The recently appointed Secretary of War, Lord Kitchener, vehemently disagreed with leaders asserting the war

A disappointed recruit.

would be over by Christmas. On 8 August, Kitchener had called for 100,000 army volunteers between the ages of 19 and 30. Within ten days, Liverpool had gained War Office permission to raise K Battalion of the King's Liverpool Regiment. Over 250 recruits had already enlisted and according to the 18 August edition of the *Liverpool Daily Post and Mercury*: 'every effort was being made to be able to report that Liverpool was the first to place a new 800 strong battalion in the field'.

More men and hospitals were urgently needed. The War Office accepted the Earl of Derby's offer

The Earl of Derby, effectively the 'king of Lancashire'.

of Knowsley Hall as a 120-bed base hospital. Not to be outdone, Mr Holbrook-Gaskell placed at the disposal of the War Office his 62-acre south Liverpool estate, comprising his fully equipped mansion Woolton Hall and Woolton Wood. The War Office also accepted the offer from the trustees of the late Sir Alfred Jones to use his Aigburth Road property Oaklands as a temporary military hospital; it sat within a 6-acre estate between Aigburth and Garston. The David Lewis Northern Hospital also placed fifty beds at the disposal of the War Office. Later in the month, Stanley Hospital offered the military authorities the use of the 'Soldiers Ward', in existence since the Boer War. As Liverpool began to gear up for an influx of battle casualties, tragic events closer to home were an indication of the horrors to come.

Louis Morrice was employed by the British American Tobacco company as a labourer. On 5 August, the 20-year-old enlisted at Sefton Park barracks; in no time he was serving as a gunner with 1st Lancashire Brigade RGA on Bidston Hill garrison duty. The sandstone ridge with a peak of 231ft (70m) is covered with 100 acres of heath and woodland and overlooks the tip of Wirral. From this strategic position the artillery acted as a look-out station for the Mersey Dock and Harbour Board and threatened to endanger enemy vessels attempting to navigate safely the Rock Channel.

Most military duties have an element of danger and a tragedy unfolded after a man passed through the Territorial unit's gun park, scaled a perimeter wall and when challenged scrambled down into the woodland. The circumstances appertaining to the 10 August death of Gunner Morrice were reported in the 13 August edition of the *Liverpool Echo*:

On Monday [shortly after midnight] an alarm was raised consequent upon the report of a sentry that a suspected person was loitering in the vicinity of the gun park. The guard turned out, and some shots were fired. Then, under the direction of Lieutenant Cook, the men split into parties, were moved through the fir wood in extended order with the object of searching for the trespasser. Morrice was one of a party of five who made their way through thick undergrowth towards the railing dividing the wood from Eleanor Road. When with two or three yards of the railing deceased's comrades saw a flash in front followed by a report. Morrice who was nearest the railings, staggered, cried 'Oh, I've been shot' and fell to the ground. It was found that a bullet had passed through his body, and although medical aid was promptly summoned, the young soldier died a few minutes after the shot had been fired.

The mysterious death formed the subject of an inquest held in the reading room of Bidston village by the West Cheshire Coroner. During the inquest it became apparent the men in the deceased's party were not in complete agreement about which direction the shot that killed Morrice had come from. The proceedings lasted almost two hours and ended in the jury recording an open verdict. They agreed that death was caused by a bullet, but there was no evidence to show who had fired the fatal shot.

On 16 August, Gunner Louis Morrice received a full military funeral at Ford Cemetery, Liverpool.

A similar tragedy occurred shortly after midnight on 12 August. Travelling salesman William Robert Dawson from Morecambe approached the Dunning's Bridge crossing of the Leeds and Liverpool canal. After failing to respond to a challenge by a sentry, the 62-year-old was shot and fatally wounded. He was taken to the nearby Maghull Epileptic Homes, but died shortly afterwards.

Meanwhile eager ladies enrolled by the Liverpool Civic Service League conducted a house to house K Battalion recruitment drive. During the 4 days prior to 21 August, 748 men had volunteered for K Battalion and a decision was made to raise the strength to the maximum of 957 men.

Headstone of Gunner Louis Morrice.

Lord Kitchener agreed to be the honorary colonel of the battalion and Lord Derby visited Seaforth Depot where he appealed for more volunteers. Three days later the 11th (Service) Battalion of the King's Liverpool Regiment gained the distinction of being the first New Army battalion. By the end of August they were in Aldershot, the following January they became a pioneer battalion.

The patriotism of the Kitchener volunteers was unquestionable, unlike that of Robert Arthur Blackburn. The 18-year-old was employed in his fathers' lodging house at 121B Islington until he was arrested under the Official Secrets Act. He appeared in the Liverpool Police Court charged with communicating information likely to be of use to His Majesty's enemies. In June the prisoner first contacted the German Embassy in London advising of his willingness to sell them secrets with regard to the Mersey Defences. He received a reply from Leo Sirius in Berlin offering payment for information concerning full details of the warships being constructed at Cammell Laird, and details of merchant ships in the port and Mersey Defences. Sirius evidently received information as he forwarded two £1 postal orders and questions about the two permanent Mersey forts, whether the harbour was protected by mines and other particulars. Following a spy alert from the War Office, police raided the prisoner's home in Jenkinson Street, where they found originals of the letters, documents and an Admiralty plan showing in detail the Formby and New Brighton coast. Blackburn professed all the information was freely available and that he meant no harm but eventually admitted the charge of communicating with the enemy and was committed for trial. At Liverpool Assizes on 28 October the youth pleaded guilty to three indictments of communicating information useful to an enemy, and then received two years' custody at a Borstal institution.

Within a fortnight 100,000 men of all social classes had responded to Kitchener's call to arms, and on 28 August, Kitchener called for a further 100,000 volunteers. A few days before, Lords Kitchener and Derby discussed and agreed to the latter's suggestion for a battalion of men raised from the commercial offices of Liverpool who would serve together as comrades. Derby's 27 August newspaper appeal resulted in 1,500 recruits from the commercial offices converging on the 5/King's drill hall. Though the signing of papers was postponed until

Monday, the pledge made by the men en masse was so unmistakably genuine a telegram was immediately despatched to Kitchener advising the battalion of pals was full.

Derby invited the assembled volunteers to report on 31 August to St George's Hall, as this relieved the recruiting pressure on the Old Haymarket office. The first battalion was raised within an hour, and continued in accordance with War Office orders until 5 September when a total of 2,865 men, almost sufficient for a trio of pals battalions, had enlisted.

On Saturday morning, Liverpool had their first opportunity of seeing the comrades en masse. After mustering in their trade sections at their respective exchanges or on Exchange Flags, the men marched through the city to Ivy Farm, Tramway Road, Aigburth where a general parade took place before their commander. After a crash course in drill, the recruits marched in four columns along thoroughfares lined with cheering crowds to be reviewed on the steps of St George's Hall by General Sir Henry Mackinnon Commander-in-Chief (CIC) Western Command and other prominent individuals excluding the incapacitated Lord Derby.

Exchange Flags.

The Pals' Barracks, Prescot.

After the review, due to a lack of accommodation the men returned home and remained on reserve until they were contacted. They each served one day with the colours and were then allowed to continue their normal employment. For the first day they received 1s 9d and until they were called up received a retainer of 6d (2½p) a day.

The acquisition of the vacant Prescot watches factory alleviated the billeting problem. The somewhat dilapidated building was thoroughly cleaned and whitewashed courtesy of the Cunard and White Star shipping company, which also provided 1,100 mattresses, while the City Caterers were entrusted with providing meals. On 14 September the 1st City Battalion and, according to the *Liverpool Courier*, the bulk of the 2nd City Battalion marched from Sefton Park to the Prescot barracks. The following day the Hooton Park Racecourse Committee offered the use of their Wirral racecourse, grounds and outbuildings for training and billets, and the 2nd City Battalion arrived on 23 September. Other recruits remained at home, reporting daily for drill in Sefton Park until hutments at Knowsley Park were constructed. Ultimately, three battalions were billeted and trained there, joined daily by the 17th Battalion who marched from their nearby Prescot billet.

Earlier in the month, the ailing Lord Derby had the satisfaction of wiring Kitchener, advising 300 daytime recruits were joined in the evening by 771 St Helens volunteers and that the 12/King's Battalion was now full. By the end of September, the 13th and 14th Battalions had also been raised, equipped and departed for Codford and Eastbourne respectively. Near the end of November the 15th and 16th Battalions had departed for Altcar and Hoylake.

Opportunities also arose for men over the military age limit of 35. The Wavertree Patriotic Rifle Corps was formed to instruct 200 men in the art of shooting at their miniature rifle range. The range was open every evening and on Saturday afternoon practice sessions were held at Wavertree quarry, in Woolton Road.

Guns of a far greater calibre were employed by the Royal Navy Grand Fleet and Germany's High Seas Fleet. The British warships may have outnumbered the German fleet but the Kaiser's vessels had superior design, weaponry and heavier armoured plates. As the summer of 1914 gave way to autumn the Royal Navy patrolled the North Sea to restrict the German High Seas Fleet, shield the east coast against

The 3rd Pals, otherwise known as the 19/King's, training in Sefton Park.

invasion, operate a distant blockade of German ports and guard the North Sea exits. Within this watery expanse the world's two largest navies feinted and parried blows in minor skirmishes, neither side wishing to expose 'castles of steel' to unnessary risk that might endanger the balance of naval seapower. However this equilibrium was threatened by the success of German naval mines and the coming of age of the submarine.

On 22 September, three obsolete British cruisers, HMS *Aboukir*, HMS *Hogue* and HMS *Cressy*, were patrolling in file off the Dutch coast unaware they were being covertly observed from the German submarine *U9*. In rapid succession Captain Lieutenant Otto Weddigen fired a series of torpedoes; the trio of targets quickly plunged to the seabed claiming 1,459 lives. The tragedy humiliated the Royal Navy; the submarine had come of age and altered forever naval tactics.

On the day of the tragedy, the Elder Dempster steamer *Eloby* brought 120 wounded British soldiers to Liverpool. This was the first time Liverpool had come into direct contact with the war. Only thirty

HMS Hogue, *one of the obsolete cruisers of the live-bait squadron.*

1914 – EAGER FOR A FIGHT 39

patients were stretcher cases, the remainder suffering from shrapnel wounds. They were taken to Fazakerley Hospital, where during the evening they were visited by the Bishop of Liverpool, Dr Chavasse. Lesser visitors were only admitted on Sundays and Wednesdays between 2.30 and 4pm on production of a one-person pass applied for in advance. The restrictions reminded the wounded they were still under military discipline. On 1 October the first train of wounded arrived at Aintree station; the ambulance trains generally arrived between 11pm and 4am.

Military law prevailed throughout the nation, and led to the fatal shooting of Frank Powell Jones of Church Road, Waterloo. The 27-year-old was described as an independent gentleman who met his death shortly after midnight on 25 September. Jones was returning from Southport on a motorcycle and a sidecar containing Mr Drew of the Queens Hotel, Waterloo. During their journey they were challenged several times by sentries and halted. On passing Little Crosby church, Drew told the County Coroner, 'I heard a report and I thought one of the tyres had burst, the sidecar ran into the kerbstone, I jumped out calling what's the matter? Several soldiers approached and informed me they had shot the rider who was now lying in the road.' Private John Finnerty, 3/King's, stated he was on sentry duty with Private Airey outside the church and in compliance with orders, he had shouted three times, 'Halt who goes there', and his colleague challenged once. The motorcycle had passed them by 20yd when the sentry fired once. Corroborative evidence was given by the other sentry and the corporal of the guard. After hearing the details of the injuries to the deceased's head and despite the absence of a red warning sentry post light, the jury recorded a verdict of justifiable homicide.

More fortunate were the latest contingent of 145 wounded who arrived at Aintree station from Southampton on the evening of 7 October. Unlike previous arrivals, the men were bright and clean-looking for they had spent several days in a French hospital. The men were mainly wounded on the first day of the Battle of Soissons. Almost 100 were able to walk, others were assisted and the 25 stretcher cases of shrapnel victims were loaded into ambulances by 50 volunteer ambulance men from Number 7 VAD. On arrival at hospital a further thirty railway first-aid assistants helped put the men to bed, usually with a comforting cigarette.

The addictive properties of tobacco are evident in a letter dated 1 October received by Lord Derby from the officer commanding the 1/KLR.

Dear Lord Derby.

The officers of the 1/KLR have seen with the greatest regret the reports in the papers of your severe indisposition. We hope that your health is now well established. We are following with the deepest interest the accounts of which Liverpool is swelling the ranks of our forces.

The battalion is I hope, upholding the honour of Liverpool. We were amongst the first troops to leave Aldershot, disembarked at Havre, took part in the big march at Mons, and the subsequent retirement to Paris, and have taken our share in the battles of the Marne and the Aisne.

We have had three officers killed and ten wounded, and 250 NCOs and men killed or wounded. We had pretty stiff fighting at Mons, Baai, Villers Colterets, Hautevevesnes, as well as the Aisne and Marne.

The people of Liverpool have been very kind to us in sending gifts, tobacco and cigarettes etc, and when in the trenches, cold, wet and hungry, with our last cigarette, and almost our last match gone, you can imagine the joy with which these gifts are received.

I understand that our Old Comrades Association is looking splendidly after our wives and families, and we are all looking forward to our next Old Comrades Dinner in Liverpool, when we shall be able to express our gratitude in person to the city of Liverpool.

Yours sincerely, W.S. Bannatyre.

The city also provided sanctuary for Belgian refugees. In mid-October, a further 400 working class Belgians from Antwerp, Malines and Louvain arrived by special train and were received at Lime Street by the Liverpool Consul for Belgium Refugees and other Allies, as the band of the 79th Brigade of Scouts played the Belgian national anthem. Vehicles took the refugees to the workhouse institutions at Belmont Road, Toxteth and Smithdown Road, where they were placed in blocks

The 19th Battalion silver badge presentation at Knowsley Hall. Lady Derby is seen handing a badge to Lord Derby.

away from the other occupants. The cost of their keep in these establishments was borne by the government until they transferred to private homes.

The historic house of Stanley received on 16 October a unique honour bestowed by George V for Lord Derby's work raising three comrades battalions. The pals were entitled to go into battle wearing on their caps the Stanley coat of arms. In recognition of this great honour Lord Derby purchased silver badges, and these were presented to every man in the battalion as a memento of the unique and historic occasion.

On the same day, the recuperating Lord Derby received a letter from Kitchener authorising the raising of a fourth pals battalion. Recruiting commenced on 14 October and after

The silver cap badge worn by the Liverpool Pals.

sluggish progress concluded on 14 November, fulfilling Derby's ambition to raise a pals brigade. The battalions were initially known as the 1st City, 2nd City, 3rd City and 4th City battalions or the 1st, 2nd, 3rd and 4th Pals. Later they were officially entitled the 17th, 18th, 19th and 20th (Service) battalions of the King's Liverpool Regiment; in 1915 the Pals 21st and 22nd (Reserve) battalions were formed.

A younger generation were also 'on war service'. In late October the fifth AGM of the Liverpool Boy Scouts Association reported they had 45 troops with a total of 2,780 scouts, with 8 church scout troops with a membership of 230 awaiting registration and 14 new troops in the making. The scouts acted as messengers at the town hall, police and fire brigade stations and assisted the Civic Service League, helped at recruiting offices, Army Service Corps Camp and Seaforth Barracks.

Also in the news were the activities of a junior lieutenant in the German Naval Reserve. Carl Hans Lody was a German spy who spoke fluent English. Travelling on a false American passport, he arrived at Newcastle on 27 August prior to visiting the Firth of Forth. He sent defensive and fleet movement information to Stockholm unaware that his messages were being intercepted by Military Intelligence, who ensured only misleading information reached its destination. Lody had decided to 'lie low' in Ireland, which required sailing on a ferry from the busy port of Liverpool. This afforded the skilled and accurate observer the opportunity to write a detailed letter describing the ships in port and other military disclosures, which unlike previous letters was of real military value to the Germans. On 29 September Lody sailed for Dublin. Postal censors intercepted his letter and MI5 ordered his arrest. He was traced to Ireland and arrested on 2 October then taken to London where he was charged with and admitted treason. On 6 November, Lody was executed by firing squad in the Tower of London.

The proof of an espionage network led the Home Office to order the round-up of German and Austrians. In two days the Metropolitan Police arrested 1,600 aliens destined for detention camps. In Liverpool the police worked day and night and arrested every German, Hungarian or Austrian male between the ages of 17 and 45, including the Liver bird sculptor Carl Bernard Bartels.

Detainees were transferred to camps at Lancaster and Queensferry, the latter established in a large disused factory enclosed by a wooden palisade. A further 4,000 aliens were detained in a camp at Douglas,

Isle of Man, where on 19 November during a disturbance, the guards opened fire. The incident claimed the lives of five prisoners and a dozen more were wounded. A far larger camp was constructed at Knockaloe near Peel, and by the end of the war the camp held almost 24,000 internees.

The relief of the wives and children of the interned aliens came from funds allocated by the German and Austrian governments and administrated by the American Embassy; however, grants were not available for British born wives and dependents. Outside of London a wife received 8s (40p) and 1s 6d for each child. There were thirty-two wives and eighty-four children in the West Derby Union being assisted in this way.

THE IDEA –
THOUGHT I WAS A BALLY ALIEN

'Bally Alien'.

Another philanthropic gesture came from Mr and Mrs Charles Williamson who vacated their mansion at Camp Hill, Woolton in early October. This was one of the city's earliest auxiliary hospitals and initially housed forty beds, later increasing to sixty. The patients were amputees transferred from Fazakerley Hospital.

The War Office also utilised the Royal Southern Hospital which made the eighty-bed Victoria Ward available for invalided soldiers, prompting immediate requests for donations in kind or money to add to the comfort of the men. Simultaneously, wounded Belgians were receiving treatment at the David Lewis Northern Hospital. In October, Mr and Mrs Richard D. Holt vacated their large detached house at 54 Ullett Road and it was equipped as an auxiliary military hospital. Throughout its three-year existence the Holts paid all the expenses.

During November the West Derby Union made available to the military the recently opened 600-bed Alder Hey Infirmary and at a later date tents capable of accommodating 300 patients were erected in the grounds. For approximately 3 months this was a general hospital, but

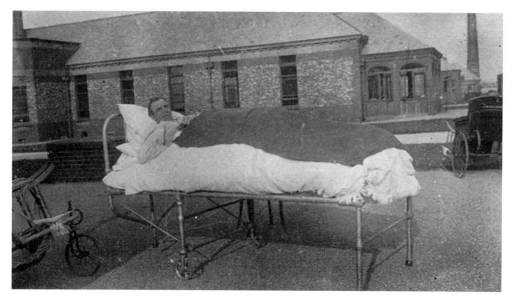

Sergeant Major Lawson taking the air at Fazakerley.

in January 1915 a section of the hospital housed 200 beds for specialist orthopaedic treatment. All the patients were referred from other British hospitals and the demand was such that within a few months the entire accommodation was devoted to orthopaedics.

A collection of temporary buildings housed X-ray facilities, the Limb Fitting Department, Electro-therapy Department and others. The hospital was an auxiliary of the 1st Western General Hospital until October 1917, when it became an independent hospital, and at this point 9,997 patients had received orthopaedic treatment. The following auxiliary hospitals were now attached to Alder Hey: Highfield Infirmary, Pilkington's Hospital, St Helens, Blackmore Hospital West Derby, Lees Wood Hall, Mold, Dawpool Hospital, Thurstaston and Wilton Grange, West Kirby. A total of 13,300 patients were treated at Alder Hey and its satellite hospitals.

The former Moss Side Institution at Maghull became a 300-bed Red Cross military hospital, benefitting from a specialist neurological ward, and the first military patient was admitted on 21 December.

The increase in medical facilities for the influx of wounded and mutilated soldiers did little to assuage the tide of patriotic volunteers.

Given the overwhelming availability of recruits, the military authorities could afford to be selective. Great numbers of erstwhile recruits were rejected on medical grounds or failure to meet the army minimum height standard of 5ft 3in (1.6m). An incident occurred in a Birkenhead recruiting office, where an undersized reject offered to fight every man in the room, leading to Alfred Bigland MP raising the Birkenhead Bantams, named after small pugnacious fighting cocks. Recruitment commenced on 30 November, and within four days two battalions of Birkenhead Bantams were raised, followed by a third depot battalion. The battalions on adoption by the War Office became the 15th, 16th (Service) and 17th (Reserve) Battalions of the Cheshire Regiment. Other towns and cities followed Birkenhead's initiative, resulting in the formation of the 35th (Bantam) Division.

The Bantams proved a novel boost to recruitment, but one of the most significant factors affecting voluntarism was an incident that occurred on 16 December 1914. A pair of German battle cruisers commenced a thirty-minute devastating and demoralising bombardment of Scarborough, resulting in seventeen civilian deaths, including a baby and several children, and eighty injured. The 'baby killers' of Scarborough then headed north, briefly shelling the fishing port of Whitby, before bombarding the garrisoned port of Hartlepool, where a further 86 civilians died, 424 were injured and 7 soldiers were killed.

Instead of the much-quoted 'The war would be over by Christmas', in reality it transpired 'the war was over here by Christmas', with no end in sight.

CHAPTER 3

1915
Deepening Conflict

In the absence of the predicted swift victory, the combatant nations faced a strategic quandary over the most advantageous location to deploy their forces. As a stalemate existed on the Western Front, Germany opted for an overtly defensive strategy in France and Flanders and concentrated on defeating Russia. The respite afforded the beleaguered Allied armies precious time to regroup and absorb inexperienced battalions. Troopships, including those from New Zealand, Australia, Canada and the Dominions, now faced an additional hazard. On 20 October the coal-carrying *Glitra* was intercepted by *U17* off the Norwegian coast. The unarmed vessel was boarded and scuttled making her the first British merchantman sunk by a German submarine.

Liverpool was the greatest transport centre at the disposal of the Allies for the transhipment of troops, munitions and foodstuffs. Almost daily horses and mules from Argentina, South Africa and Canada arrived. Most of them passed through Liverpool's Canada Dock and landing stage destined for the largest army remount department in the country. The Earl of Lathom (serving with the Lancashire Hussars) had placed Lathom Park at the disposal of the War Office. For almost 3 months 1,000 workers had constructed a depot comprising several hundred corrugated stables and huts all mounted on concrete bases. The site could accommodate 7,000 horses and 1,500 grooms. On completion of their 15-mile journey from Riverside station, horses were

Remount horses being unloaded at Ormskirk station.

unloaded at Ormskirk station and driven on the hoof the few miles to the depot.

By early January a branch line had been laid into the depot, which had already dealt with 40,000 equines. During the war, some 223,000 horses and mules passed through Riverside station with over 24,000 wagons used to transport these animals. No fewer than 500 special trains were run, and if all the wagons were coupled together, they would have extended from Liverpool to Windermere.

Passengers also used Riverside station including the German survivors of the 8 December British naval victory off the Falkland Islands. On 14 January 180 prisoners from the *Gneisenau*, 12 from the *Nurnberg* and a few from the *Leipzig* passed through Riverside station and boarded a special south-bound train. They had only the briefest stay in the port where 42 steamers were waiting for unloading berths, the delay being due to 8,000 dock workers, equivalent to 1 in 4, having enlisted. The remaining men were members of the Dock Labourers Union which refused to accept replacement workers between 20 and 30 years deemed eligible for military service, others lacked experience and the work took longer. The difficulties were compounded by the large volume of work diverted to the port and considerable railway congestion.

The relationship between most employers and employees was exceedingly poor, not helped by soaring inflation and the price of fish, bread and meat being at record levels. On the home front, the difference between life and death was becoming increasingly arbitrary, the latest example of 'Hun frightfulness' occurring on 19 January when Zeppelin airships carried out their first successful bombing raid on Britain, and more followed.

In response to civilian disquiet over German raids, the Royal Navy answered with a 24 January victory at the Battle of Dogger Bank. This curtailed the German naval raids, but evidence of poor naval gunnery and ineffectual communications was again ignored.

However, three days later two merchant ships were torpedoed without warning by *U20*, and in doing so the old-fashioned courtesy of preserving life at sea fell by the wayside. On the penultimate day of the month a dramatic stroke brought the war to Liverpool. The German submarine *U21* appeared between Morecambe and northwest of the Mersey Bar and sank two British ships, the *Ben Cruachan* and the *Linda Blanche*. Both crews were given ten minutes to abandon ship prior to the detonation of explosives placed deep in the hull, and an unidentified third vessel was reported sunk. In the early morning light, the Belfast to Liverpool steamer *Graphic* arrived in an area strewn with wreckage, and sailed towards a distressed ship almost 4 miles away, as recorded by Captain Porter:

> Suddenly with a dull boom, the steamer disappeared among the waves, making her exit amid dense clouds of smoke. When the steam had cleared away I saw through my glasses a dark object lying low in the water shaped like a long whale. The light improved slightly at this moment. The submarine immediately came in our direction, we changed course and headed into the wind disadvantaging the submarine in the choppy sea the submarine pursued us for thirty minutes and gradually fell far behind.

The Western Approaches would become a graveyard of merchant ships and Liverpool mercantile marine personnel. Britain's distant economic naval blockade of Germany was beginning to bite. On 1 February, Germany announced an unrestricted submarine campaign, and henceforth ships of any nationality would be sunk without warning. This was soon followed by the German declaration that the waters around the British Isles were a war zone.

A U-boat commander watches his victim plunge to the seabed.

All too aware of the consequences of a deepening conflict were the British Red Cross Society, who visualised a shortage of hospital accommodation. In November, Mr R. Burton Chadwick attended a London meeting on the subject, and he returned to Liverpool determined to persuade his fellow citizens to provide £13,000 for an overseas base hospital and £1,500 a month running costs. On 14 November, a meeting was convened in the Exchange News Room, Liverpool, during which a powerful appeal was delivered for the establishment of an overseas hospital wholly administered, equipped, staffed and maintained by the Liverpool Chamber of Commerce. The proposal was favourably received and promises of donations and subscriptions for what became the Liverpool Merchants' Hospital were showered on the promoters. An administrative council was formed and plans were drawn up for a fully equipped hospital comprising eight pavilion wards, each accommodating twenty-six patients, with their own nurses' duty rooms, sink, stores, bath and toilet. The mobile hospital, complete with operating theatre and X-ray equipment, was optimistically designed to be dismantled or erected within one hour so it could follow the expected Allied advance to the Rhine. The mobility element increased construction costs and inevitably posed a challenge for the architect, Mr T. E. Eccles; the construction and erection was assigned to Tomkinson of Liverpool. From 22 February two of the wards, operating theatre and administration offices were temporarily erected in Ullett Road playground, where visitors paid a small entrance fee towards funds.

The non-combatant visitors also had a slim chance of death from enemy action, as evidenced by the air attacks or naval bombardment plaguing parts of the nation. On Saturday, 13 February, by order of the general commanding port defences, air-raid precaution lighting regulations were instigated, public illuminations were dimmed to half their brightness and buildings and places aircraft navigators would be anxious to locate were left in total darkness. The clocks on the Liver Building, other illuminated clocks and bright motor car headlights were prohibited. The *Liverpool Echo* reported:

The Admiralty War Service badge was introduced on 16 February 1915 for shipyard munition workers; the date remained unaltered throughout the war.

> Lord Street and Church Street, thronged as they always are on a Saturday night with arm-linked promenaders and people hurrying to and fro theatres, had an air of unwanted glumness. The big arc lights were out, and the only lights were those in the small coupled globes, halfway up the standards. Lime Street took on an eerie character in the partial eclipse.

Church Street, Liverpool.

Meanwhile, on the Western Front, the arrival of spring stirred the Allies into action. On 10 March the British attacked the Germans defending the French village of Neuve Chapelle. Indian and British troops including the 1/King's and some 1/5 King's attacked on a 4,000yd frontage capturing the village and several lines of trenches. But a shortage of artillery shells and German counter-attacks prevented a breakthrough, and after 3 days the battle died away as the captured ground gained at the expense of 11,500 casualties was consolidated. The *Liverpool Echo* reported 219 dead from the 1/King's and 119 wounded during the assault. It can only be conjectured if any of the above wounded were treated at Merseyside's latest auxiliary hospitals.

In late February, The Tower Hospital at Rainhill founded by St Helens 40 VAD came into operation when thirty-four invalid comrades were transferred from Prescot. A recent appeal by Mr G. A. Cassady, the Mayor of Bootle, on behalf of Number 14 VAD raised the required £600, and the executors of the late Mr R. J. Glasgow lent his Breeze Hill, Bootle property for hospital use. It was officially opened on 13 March by Archdeacon Spooner.

The next day, VAD 40 also opened 'Oakdene', a large private house in Rainhill loaned by Henry Gamble. The thirty-bed Class A auxiliary hospital was capable of receiving patients direct from ambulance trains.

In February the Women's War Service Bureau, now in possession of St John Ambulance certificates, was accepted as 58 VAD. In March they began three months' training in the Royal Infirmary where they attended twice a week for a mere three hours. Financing the diverse range of community run hospitals or nursing homes proved something of a financial headache, and despite the War Office hospital accommodation payment of 2*s* per bed, per day, appeals of every description became commonplace.

The Women's War Service Bureau also recognised the need for a central buffet for soldiers and sailors passing through Liverpool on their way to and from the front or fleet. Adjoining the entrance to Lime Street station were spacious empty premises, originally a hotel. The property belonged to Moss Empires whose original Empire Theatre was next door to 11 Lime Street. The proprietors placed 11 Lime Street at the disposal of the women, financed the conversion, assisted in furnishing the establishment and organised dedicated fundraising matinees. The Cunard and White Star Lines supplied most of the kitchen equipment. There was a large dining room, a comfortable lounge with piano, a writing room and four billiard tables. The Lime Street Soldiers' and Sailors' Club was opened 16 March by Lady Sefton and remained in existence until 17 June 1919. Originally, the club opened for twelve hours daily, but the following January the hours were greatly increased to facilitate the reception of bona-fide travellers. From March 1915 to early November 1916 the club had 314,460 military visitors.

Another military visitor was about to intervene in the ongoing Merseyside dock workers' dispute. On Sunday, 21 March, despite religious leaders objecting to the review being held on the Sabbath, the Secretary of State for War, Lord Kitchener, fleetingly attended morale-boosting martial reviews in Liverpool and Manchester. From the steps of St George's Hall, Kitchener, Lord Derby, Alfred Bigland, civic dignitaries and military staff officers reviewed 12,000 locally raised New Army troops. The sun shone brightly on the parade led by twelve men representing the partly recruited Lancashire Divisional Artillery, followed by four battalions of the Comrades Brigade, 14/Cheshire, 10/South Lancashire, 16/King's and the Lilliputian bantams of the 15th and 16/Cheshires, all watched by 100,000 spectators.

Lord Kitchener, Liverpool, Sunday, 21 March 1915.

Before leaving for Manchester, Kitchener held a brief meeting with the Merseyside leaders of the National Union of Dock Labourers. Kitchener impressed most forcefully the dangers that were being caused by congestion of work at the docks, a situation aggravated by the refusal of a section of employees to work overtime during the week and Saturday. Kitchener then bid farewell for a similar review in Manchester.

Four days later, at midnight another special train departed Liverpool carrying most of the Liverpool Merchants' Hospital staff and tons of equipment destined for Étaples, some 18 miles south of Boulogne.

The home-front infrastructure may have been progressing nicely but British industry responded lethargically to the clamour for artillery

The St George's Plateau military review of local troops.

shells. In some quarters excessive alcohol consumption was deemed responsible for poor output, adding a further reason for those advocating temperance or prohibition of alcohol. Following *The Times* reporting of the Neuve Chapelle shell shortage, the pressure applied by the Conservative Party brought about the collapse of the Liberal government. The new coalition government established a Ministry of Munitions under the auspices of David Lloyd George. On 21 April he stated:

> During the fortnight of fighting in and around Neuve Chapelle almost as much ammunition was spent by our artillery as during the whole of the two and three quarter years of the Boer War. The urgent need for the country, then, is for shells, shells and more shells. . . . A radical change of organization is necessary and it must be carried out at once.

Lloyd George was also a long-term supporter of the temperance movement. In March 1915 he famously stated, 'We are fighting Germany, Austria and drink'.

Lloyd George had no shortage of supporters, and a few weeks earlier Wesleyan ministers had protested against a whisky advert on Liverpool tram tickets. Drinkers were dealt a blow when the Commander-in-Chief of Western Command implemented DORA regulations. After 29 March all licensed premises (whether for consumption on or off the premises) could only open between 10.30am and 10pm. Sunday hours were between 12.30pm and 2.30pm and between the hours of 6.30pm and 9.00pm. It was hoped the reduced hours would curtail absenteeism and therefore reduce port congestion, a matter on which Lord Derby had given considerable thought.

At the beginning of April, Lord Derby chaired a meeting of dock workers and proposed they join a military style battalion of dock workers commanded by him. The Khaki Dockers Battalion comprised men over military age and was to concentrate on government work, reduce congestion in the port and provide men with an opportunity to serve their country. They were offered normal rates of pay plus an army payment. Despite a favourable response, only a fraction of the men attending the mass meeting could be employed in the small pilot scheme. In the second week of April, 350 men reported for duty at the battalion's Regent Road headquarters. They were issued with military style khaki overalls and learnt the rudiments of military deportment. Military discipline was asserted by 6ft 3in tall Regimental Sergeant Major Patrick McKibbins, a former 1/Scots Guardsman who was injured during the Mons Retreat. The nucleus of labourers became the forerunners of the 1st and 2nd Dock Battalions of the King's Liverpool Regiment. No man was accepted unless he belonged to, and continued to be a member of, the Dock Workers Trade Union. Military and trade-union rules applied, including an agreement that the battalion was not to be used in a strike-breaking role. Attempts to implement the scheme at Birkenhead failed for a considerable period, although other ports did introduce dock battalions.

Across the Channel, the erection of the Liverpool Merchants' Hospital   at the ancient fishing village of Étaples encountered considerable delays due to the inadequacies of the local elderly labour. Meanwhile, the medical staff set up 4 large wards and operating and X-ray rooms in the Grand Hotel and Casino de la Page in Paris Plage, 'a fashionable watering-place near Calais'; some 750 patients received treatment there. Accounts differ on the inauguration of the mobile

Lord Derby inspecting the Dock Workers Battalion.

hospital, but the *Daily Post and Mercury* reported during the week ending 28 April that four convoys were received. Admissions during the week amounted to 172, and the total admitted since the hospital had opened was 277.

As the casualties mounted, the Allies attempted to break the Western Front impasse by controversially launching an Anglo-French campaign against the Turkish army at Gallipoli. Anglo-French warships attempted to force the Dardanelles strait to open up the supply route to Russia's Black Sea ports, but they suffered a humiliating defeat. On 25 April, the Allies made amphibious landings on the Gallipoli shores, but bedevilled from the outset by inept leadership the campaign ultimately became a military fiasco.

Meanwhile, on the Western Front, near Ypres, the Germans deployed their latest example of frightfulness – poison gas; but their attempt to break the deadlock failed. Throughout the year the British attempted to wrest insignificant villages from the German invader, the battlefields of Loos, Neuve Chapelle and the Ypres salient rapidly attained their own notoriety to the war weary soldiers awaiting reinforcement by Kitchener's New Army. In Liverpool aspersions were

RMS Lusitania *alongside Liverpool landing stage.*

directed at 'Derby's Lapdogs', comfortably ensconced at Knowsley. The matter was resolved on 30 April when the Pals battalions entrained for Belton Camp at Grantham, Lincolnshire. But, it would still be early November before the Liverpool Pals, a component of 89 Division of the 30th Division, proceeded to France.

Imperilled from the outset of hostilities were the underrated Merseyside men, women and boys of the Mercantile Marine who in war or peace sailed the high seas. Some of the most illustrious shipping companies were based in Liverpool, including Cunard whose 30,000-ton transatlantic liner RMS *Lusitania* regularly steamed between New York and Liverpool. The liner held the Blue Riband for the fastest crossing of the Atlantic by a passenger vessel (four-and-a-half days) and was confident in her ability to outrun any surfaced hostile submarine. On Friday, 7 May, as the vessel sailed 15 miles off the Irish coast, *Lusitania* was torpedoed by the German submarine *U20*. The liner sank in minutes, with 1,198 souls perishing including 124 American citizens.

The *Liverpool Daily Post* reported:

The deep feeling of resentment aroused by the sinking of the *Lusitania* was marked in Liverpool on Saturday and Sunday nights by an unrestrained wrecking and looting of German shops in the city. In the north-end where seafaring men mostly reside, the outbreak of hostility towards German residents and shopkeepers was so determined the police were powerless to check the depredations of indignant people. Pork butchers shops [three-quarters in the city had German owners] were wrecked systematically from Mile End to Rice Lane, a distance of two miles. It took the police by surprise and a great deal of damage was done before they were able to stem the tide of destruction.

Cunard notified the families that the *Lusitania* survivors would return home by train. Long before dawn on 9 May the families gathered at Lime Street station, with the train arriving at 6.25am. The *Daily Post and Mercury* reported:

There were also hundreds of women with heavier heads, no tidings had reached them of their men folk but they had come to scan the faces of the home-comers, with hope, hand in hand with despair. . . . The fortunate wives clutched their husbands convulsively and wept for joy . . . Side by side with these touching incidents was a tragic and heart rendering spectacle.

A quick change of front proved to no avail.

A QUICK CHANGE OF FRONT.

Other women were making a search for relatives who were not to be found. Up and down the platform they hastened, and at last they walked away for the last time, their heads bowed with the grief of realization. Shipmates had told them of the fate of their husbands and that testimony and the absence of their names from the survivors list sealed the tragedy . . .

On Monday, the riots continued against supposed Teutonic shops or any foreign-named business – furniture dealers, hairdressers, outfitters and jewellers windows were smashed with bricks, and stock hurled into the road or looted. Upstairs living areas were ransacked and furniture chucked into the street and burnt. Shops in Stanley Road, and Marsh Lane, Bootle and elsewhere were also pillaged along with stores in Litherland. Rioting also occurred in Wallasey, Birkenhead and London.

The Liverpool rioting continued on Tuesday but the trail of destruction was not as great. In the Smithdown Road and Lodge Lane district women were seen going home with their aprons filled with pork and bacon. The first fifty rioters soon appeared in court where the men, women and boys were charged with theft of flour, pork, furniture and wilful damage to windows. Several sentences of twenty-one days' hard labour were passed, while others were fined 20s (£1) with time to pay, or ordered to pay the damage.

The traumatised riot victims received no compassion and instead the authorities removed them for their own protection to the main Bridewell (police cells) in Cheapside. The Germans were reported as being 'only too grateful to be sheltered from the mob'. On 12 May, 150 aliens were taken in Black Marias (prison vans) to a cordoned off and guarded Lime Street station where they left for Hawick, Scotland; 3 days later another 150 aliens followed them. On 19 May another 72 alien shopkeepers were escorted to the landing stage and sailed for internment on the Isle of Man. Most of the city shopkeepers of alien extraction were now interned.

Almost eighty of the internees' spouses and offspring sought refuge in the local workhouses. Those with money paid their keep and half of the cost of keeping the destitute came from the earlier mentioned Austrian and German scheme.

But there was no aid for German-born Anton Kuepfiele who now

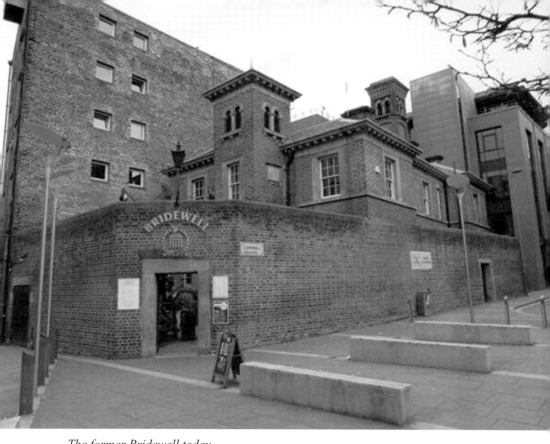

The former Bridewell today.

A propeller from the liner forms the Lusitania *memorial at the Albert Dock.*

held an American passport. He was charged with attempting to communicate to Germany information regarding British warships and military forces. On 4 February, he had left New York on the White Star liner *Arabic* and reached Liverpool ten days later. Throughout the voyage he recorded the movements or positions of warships. On 15 February he stayed in a Liverpool hotel where he wrote on business headed paper a letter to New York blissfully unaware he was under surveillance. The innocuous letter was intercepted by the Censors Office at Salisbury House and under examination was found to contain secret messages written between the lines. After a brief respite in Dublin, he went to London were he met fellow spies Muller and Hahn, who were also being shadowed. Kuepfiele attempted to book a cross-Channel passage, but sailings were temporarily suspended.

After returning to his hotel near Victoria Kuepfiele was arrested, as were his associates. A search of the hotel room revealed matching business headed paper, an iron nib pen and two lemons (the juice can be used as invisible ink). There was also a bottle of formalin which when it is applied to paper it turns invisible writing brown. Faced with the damming evidence Kuepfiele admitted he was a German spy. Due to his American nationality he was tried in a civil court where a guilty verdict would result in hanging instead of a firing squad.

For security reasons the Old Bailey trial was held in camera, but two days into the trial on the night of 20 May, Kuepfiele took his life in his Brixton prison cell. A long message on a slate included, 'He had a fair trial, but was a soldier and wished to die a soldier. I cannot bear to mount the scaffold as a spy.' Ironically, his two co-conspirators were executed by firing squad. The eleventh and final First World War spy execution on home soil occurred in April 1916.

The spy stories did little to assuage a fear of invasion. In September 1915, a move to standardise the hundreds of ad hoc drilling associations began. A central committee was formed, and a few weeks later the Central Association of Volunteer Training Corps (VTC) under the presidency of Lord Desborough emerged and was recognised by the War Office. The VTC were self-financing and recruits were obliged to purchase their own uniforms, ideally lovat green in colour as up until then volunteers on military duty wore a red armlet bearing GR for '*Georgius Rex*'.

'This way to the Volunteer Training Corps Headquarters.'

On 19 February at Liverpool Town Hall a new committee arranged the formation of the City of Liverpool Volunteer Guard. This would be in association with Desborough's VTC and incorporate the existing local drilling corps and any future ones; Colonel Forbes Bell (late Liverpool Scottish) was appointed commander. The VTC men were ineligible for the Regular and Territorial forces on account of age or some genuine reason, and each recruit had to serve for the duration of the war. Recruits completed a special VTC enrolment form, on which clause seven alluded to conscription by 'signing an undertaking he will enlist into the army if called to do so'. The Wavertree Rifle Corps' persistent objection to clause seven resulted in an amendment, 'No recruit could be bound to serve a greater distance than ten miles from Liverpool town hall' and the corps agreed to affiliation.

By early May, more than a dozen separate local drilling associations existed, and after the merger the Liverpool Guard would comprise 2,500 men equipped with 500 single-shot Martini Henry rifles. The committee selected a distinctive uniform in grey-green cloth, with rank and file members wearing puttees and a slouch hat adorned with a star badge. Army titles were forbidden, and the officers under the commandant were called company, platoon or section leaders. As the majority of men were unable to afford uniforms, the council gave an inadequate £1,000 grant, leading to public appeals for finances.

A blue and gold enamel lapel badge issued to the City of Liverpool Volunteer Guard.

Also affiliated to the VTC were the Blundellsands VTC, the Waterloo Civilian Association and St Leonard's Volunteers Bootle. On 23 May, they were inspected by Colonel Dundonald Cochrane at the West Lancashire Golf Club, Blundellsands. There were 200 men of 'smart soldierly appearance', armed with service or dummy rifles, parading as one company. After a march past they set off in attack formations across the broken ground of the golf links showing their ability to take cover from hostile fire.

Highfield Military Hospital.

A ward in Highfield Military Hospital.

Overseas, others were less fortunate and incurred severe wounds. In May a shortage of bed space led to the military authorities requesting the Select Vestry (Parish of Liverpool) to provide suitable hospital premises. The board placed Highfield Infirmary in Knotty Ash at their disposal. It was built on the separate pavilions system; each of the eight pavilions contained thirty beds.

Within forty-eight hours the patients were evacuated, and the Vestry gave the chairman 'a freehand to purchase anything that could be found to ameliorate the suffering of those patients suffering from the effects of gas'. To begin with 400 patients were accommodated, later rising to 480. Each Thursday, a large hall served as a theatre where the military patients were entertained by music-hall artistes.

Also in May, the Guardians of the Toxteth Union made available 109 beds for the treatment of servicemen at their Smithdown Road Infirmary.

The modern 900-bed Mill Road Infirmary was established to treat severe cases of sickness among West Derby residents. From 15 July, the hospital managers, the Guardians of West Derby Union, placed 700 beds at the disposal of the military. This was on the proviso that they were used solely for seriously sick or wounded servicemen, and hospital management should be left in control of the Board and existing medical staff and nursing staff remained in charge of the work.

Patients from ward E4, Mill Road Military Hospital.

An equally impressive contribution came from the City Tramways Committee when it offered to place the Lambeth Road tram-car building and repair works at the disposal of David Lloyd George, Minister of Munitions. This led to a London meeting with Lloyd George who accepted the first municipal works in the country to be offered and suggested the works be utilised for the turning of shells supplied from government casting shops. On 6 June Lloyd George and his advisors came to Liverpool and consulted with a small committee from prominent engineering firms and business brains on how Liverpool could meet War Office requirements. Lloyd George stated, 'We want rifles, we want guns, and we want shells, fuses, chemicals, and explosives. There is one thing we do want less of than usual, and that is red tape.'

By mid-June the Liverpool Munitions Committee was formed and approved, and operated from loaned offices at 325 Royal Liver Building. Machine shops throughout the country were scoured for lathes and related machinery and the larger machines from the Engineering Facility at Liverpool University were

David Lloyd George MP.

loaned. Within a month over twenty local firms were engaged in shell manufacture.

The forerunner was the City Tramways' Lambeth Road factory, now officially known in Liverpool as the First National Shell Factory. A shortage of the required machine tools for the manufacture of shells led to the general manager, on behalf of the Ministry of Munitions, borrowing about sixty lathes from local companies and manufacturing centres further afield; the Tramway's Department also loaned tooling to the Ministry. On 21 June, shell production commenced and at first the machinists at the non-profit-making factory were volunteers instructed by skilled tramway employees.

The Ministry of Muntions, who controlled the National Factories, also established a Bond Room and Inspection Department for the locally manufactured shells. The first bond of 18-pounder High Explosive (HE) shells was completed at Lambeth Road, and delivered to and passed by the inspection

Heading 18-pounder Quick Firing Cartridge Cases.

department on 20 October 1915. They were the first shells finished and passed by any of the National Shell Factories in the Lancashire region and despite the workers' inexperience, not one shell was rejected. The factory continued to increase production, and at the end of July was manufacturing 2,000 18-pounder HE shells per week. This progress continued and would have carried on if sufficient machinery had been provided, but the factory's output peaked at 20,000 18-pounder shells per week.

Women workers were employed from December 1915. The works became recognised as an exemplary production unit where people from all over the country were instructed in shell manufacture. Workers benefitted from a modern canteen offering inexpensive and wholesome meals. Musical entertainment was also provided; relations between workers and management were harmonious. The total outlay on the factory and machinery amounted to only £23,000, and the cost of production was remarkably low. The government paid outside contractors between 8 and 9s for each 18-pounder HE shell, whereas a shell produced from start to finish at Lambeth Road cost only 2s 2d.

Between July 1915 and the 1918 Armistice, the factory completely manufactured, or rectified and completed for outside contractors, the following numbers of shells:

18-pounder HE	1,906,380
4.5 HE	185,696
2.75 HE	40,850
60-pounder HE	6,569
15-pounder HE	1,795
TOTAL	2,141,290

As a further result of the Lloyd George meeting, it was decided that a Liverpool Corporation Shell Factory should be established capable of producing 20,000 18-pounder shells a week. Sir Charles Petrie set up a 'private body' committee to utilise the corporation resources for the good of the nation. However, the financial arrangements were the responsibility of the committee and the Ministry of Munitions.

In view of the urgency for shells, the committee decided no time should be wasted in erecting a factory, and instead the North Haymarket agricultural hall would be adapted. The Markets Committee immediately agreed to the loan of the premises, and on the same June day the preparing of foundations and shafting support began. The construction of a typical workshop evolved around the 60ft lengths of tram rails used, and additional corporation resources, scrap metal, shafting, machines and electric motors were utilised, together with loaned lathes. Council employees unselfishly worked long hours and shrugged off the necessity for sleep. Exactly one week after entering the building, the committee, accompanied by Lord Derby, toured the factory which was fully equipped with fifteen lathes and associated machinery.

North Haymarket Munitions Factory, 22 June 1915. The tram-line girders are noticeable.

As shell material, drawings and machine gauges were unavailable, the time was spent training male machinists and equipping machines with the special tooling required for assorted processes. As soon as the deficient items were available production commenced. In the early months, a considerable number of businessmen gave their services, especially for night work, until sufficient women operatives had been trained. Despite the ad hoc workforce, by the end of December, the North Haymarket National Shell Factory had a weekly output of over 4,000 18-pounder HE shells and preliminary work commenced in the manufacture of 4.5 and 6in HE shells.

Representatives of the Munitions of War Committee toured the district looking for appropriate munition factory premises. The Cunard Shipping Company had a suitable three-storey brick warehouse in Rimrose Road, Bootle housing fittings and furniture removed from their ships serving as armed merchant cruisers. After negotiations with Cunard, it was agreed they would clear the warehouse and establish and manage on behalf of the committee a non-profit-making shell

The Cunard National Shell Factory, Rimrose Road, Bootle.

factory. A leading light in this works was Superintendent Engineer Mr Galbraith and his brother, the works manager.

But, before production could begin machinery would need installing. The boring bars connected with the production of one shell were made from the piston rods of the old Cunard liner *Lucania*. Special equipment was also provided for the benefit of the predominately female workforce, who for the first time in engineering history were to undertake the production of 6in and 8in shells entirely on their own. The Cunard National Shell Factory began production in June 1915.

The Liverpool Munitions of War Committee was also involved with the small Chester National Shell Factory that machined 2.75in, 15-pounder and 18-pounder shells to be completed at Lambeth Road. They also oversaw a similar factory at Wrexham until the North Wales Board of Management was formed.

The shells were made to stringent machining tolerances but there was a national shortage of inspection gauges. Locally the problem was solved by women from the university who made the gauges after taking over the premises and equipment of the Technical Engineering Company in Clyde Street, Bootle.

Some of the firepower for the projectiles, Trinitrotoluene (TNT), an explosive used in detonators, was produced in Litherland in a factory adjacent to the tar distillers Brotherton and Company, the site is now a supermarket. The 11-acre site, 'which flared and seethed and reeked with poisonous vapours', was according to Siegfried Sassoon only a few hundred yards away from the 3/RWF camp based at Litherland, where thousands of troops of the Mersey Defence Force were in training or rehabilitating after convalescence. The site was managed by Brotherton and Company and opened in November 1914, and His Majesty's Explosive Factory Litherland was nationalised in March 1916.

Another essential component was produced by the Automatic Telephone Manufacturing Company, Edge Lane, which eventually produced 30,000 shell fuses weekly, and upwards of 2.75 million fuses were produced there for the Ministry of Munitions. As the war progressed, the company produced gun-sight mountings, field telephones and anti-submarine hydro phones.

Women workers drilling and assembling fuses.

At this stage most munitions factories were male-dominated, and the war workers were not discernible from men avoiding military service. The 'shirkers', scorned at every opportunity, drew the attention of indignant ladies who would present a white feather (a Victorian symbol of cowardice) or shower the stay-at-home in white chicken feathers; unfortunately male munitions workers received the same treatment. To prevent the social castigation of those 'doing their bit', in early 1915, the government issued a 45mm-high oval brass lapel badge to male Ministry of Munitions workers. In late June, a munitions enrolment bureau opened for two hours daily in St George's Hall, and each over military age workman enrolling received a certificate to prove he was doing his bit.

The On War Service munition badge.

The contribution of the proactive members of the Civic Service League was unquestionable. They possessed two donated ambulances and required more for transporting the wounded from station to hospital. An appeal for funds for ten ambulances was so successful that within five days sufficient donations had been received to purchase fifteen vehicles at a cost of £350 each. The glorified vans were all built to the specification of Sir James Barr. On 18 June, to mark the centenary of the Battle of Waterloo, the seventeen vehicles numbered one to eighteen, number thirteen being omitted, were drawn up along the Town Hall railings and ceremoniously presented to the city.

But more ambulances were needed as a result of the rising numbers of incapacitated servicemen and the increasing number of hospitals. George H. Melly, the co-managing director of the shipping company Lamport and Holt Line, contacted Sir James Barr advising his willingness to fund a military hospital.

In May, the Myrtle Street Sheltering Homes for Destitute Children had sent seventy waifs permanently to Canada, and numbers fell between spring and autumn. The main building was offered for hospital use as the sheltering could continue from the smaller adjoining 1 Sugnall Street. The main home was taken over as a military hospital on 5 July 1915. George H. Melly undertook to equip and maintain the hospital

The Sheltering Home for Destitute Children and adjoining Sugnall Street property.

for five years, receiving only the government grant of 2*s*, but due to inflation this was later increased nationally to 3*s* 3*d*. On 26 July, after extensive structural alterations, the 150-bed VAD hospital opened creating more work opportunities for women.

No. 1 Sugnall Street.

On either side of the front entrance to the Myrtle Street Sheltering Home are two commemorative tablets commemorating old boys of the home who came over with Canadian divisions and laid down their lives in the First World War.

The government now appealed for women to register at a Labour Exchange for paid industrial, agricultural and other employment. This delighted the National Union of Women's Suffrage Societies who suspended all political work at the outbreak of the war. Traditional roles were being challenged and changed. Since May, the LNWR had replaced enlisted Lime Street staff with female ticket collectors.

There was a further breakthrough in female emancipation in late August when

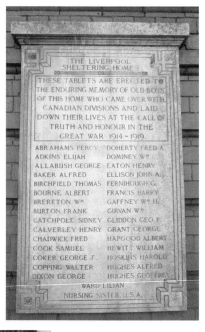

One of the Sheltering Home memorial tablets.

A women booking clerk at a railway station.

Liverpool employed sixty post women in the Wavertree and Lark Lane area. This successful experiment resulted in the employment of over 200 post ladies and the introduction of Royal Mail women drivers.

New opportunities continued to be made available to women, but the male exodus had slowed. Faced with waning recruitment, the military requested men previously rejected due to weak eyesight, defective teeth or slight physical defects to resubmit themselves for medical examination. It's probable some of the rejected men were part of the Bootle VTC, whose first muster was held in the 7/King's Park Street drill hall on the evening of 13 July.

A few days later, British Red Cross Society (BRCS) representatives met in Liverpool Town Hall to review organisations including the St John Ambulance, West Lancashire Territorial Nursing Committee, the Civic Service League and the Soldiers and Sailors Club, which in the absence of a Liverpool Red Cross had undertaken humanitarian work. The BRCS would relieve the Civic Service League from their reception of hospital ship patients. Funding would come from a subscription of a guinea for full membership or 5s for associate membership and collection boxes in banks, shops, etc. It was unanimously agreed there should be a Liverpool BRCS to coordinate resources given the fifteen military hospitals were shortly to be increased by the addition of seven schools. There would then be upwards of 9,000 beds available and transferring the military patients would require a fleet of 50 ambulances.

From the beginning of 1915, part of Woolton Convalescent Home had 100 military beds available, and between March and April 93 soldiers and sailors were treated.

Totally unexpected casualties were 22-year-old Mrs Amy Disley, Herbert her husband, sister-in-law and father-in-law as a result of an accident at 40 Redrock Street, West Derby. Mrs Campbell who lived in Redrock Street, almost opposite the Disleys, had a son who was a chauffeur at the front. He was driving 'somewhere in France' when a German Aviatik aircraft attacked the vehicle, and struck it with a bomb which failed to explode. The chauffeur, under the misconception he had rendered safe the bomb, sent it home as a war souvenir to his family. On Friday and Saturday, 30 July, the 18in (45cm) long bomb, weighing 2lb, was shown around the neighbourhood. On Saturday night the bomb slipped from the hands of Mrs Disley and exploded. She received the full blast and was mortally injured, dying shortly afterwards. Her husband and the father-in-law sustained shrapnel wounds and her sister-in-law's injuries resulted in the amputation of an arm. The coroner commented on the danger of war souvenirs circulating within the city.

The city was producing a weekly average of 400 volunteers, a far cry from the euphoria of the previous summer. Compulsory military

Officials carrying out the National Registration.

service looked inevitable and measures were introduced to determine how many young men were avoiding military service. In late July, officials door-stepped the heads of families and instructed them on how to complete the registration forms; those failing to comply were heavily fined. Commencing on 16 August, 800 volunteer Liverpool enumerators, having previously distributed, began collecting some 500,000 completed forms. The corporation were responsible for the Liverpool National Registration details, and these were collated for the government in the university offices. In mid-September the census details showed nearly 5 million males of military age were avoiding front-line service, and of these some 1½ million 'starred' men were (for now) in essential war work.

Government departments also monitored war-time production levels and attributed alcohol as the prime factor in high absenteeism and loss of output. They had considered introducing the contentious prohibition of alcohol, instead the alcoholic content of beer was reduced and shorter licensing hours were implemented. The Central Control Board issued an order for Liverpool and Lancashire districts curtailing hours when intoxicating liquor could be sold in the Mersey area. At the start of August the pubs opened at noon, closed at 2.30pm and re-opened at 6.30 until 9.30pm. Off-licences had even shorter hours, and the restrictions remained hardly unaltered until a couple of decades ago. The regulation also prohibited persons 'treating' by buying another an alcoholic drink and credit was disallowed. From 15 August, it became an offence under DORA for licensed premises to supply intoxicating alcohol to any NCO or soldier who was a patient of any military or auxiliary hospital in Western Command; this was intended to aid the quicker return of the wounded to the front.

At the forefront of humanitarian work was the Young Men's Christian Association (YMCA), which began carrying out good works with Liverpool's poorest working class in 1846. In 1877, they opened at 50–60 Mount Pleasant the first purpose-built YMCA hostel in the world. Throughout the war they provided huts for servicemen, where they could have meals, non-alcoholic drinks, write or have letters home written for them, relax or play games. Prior to June 1915, a YMCA hut existed at the army camp sited near Beech Road Schools in Litherland. A hut at Canada Dock provided primarily for the Khaki Dockers proved

Mount Pleasant YMCA.

so successful that in mid-August another five hut canteens appeared on the dock-sides.

Hundreds of Liverpool women were involved in the Women's War Service Bureau, formed on 7 August 1914. In a year their clothing and equipment department provided 249,000 articles of clothing, food and hospital requests. Included within this number were 20,000 shirts and 36,000 pairs of socks, but it excluded second-hand clothes and thousands of cigarettes. About 45,000 bandages were made in their Gambier Terrace depot.

Arrangements were also being made in all districts for shell production but there was a shortage of skilled labour in Liverpool. Some skilled men were released from their military duties to meet the required ratio of one skilled man to every ten unskilled workers.

Under the Munitions of War Act 1915, the attendance and productivity of all munitions workers was continually monitored. The first Liverpool sitting of the fortnightly Munitions Tribal aimed at promptly settling disputes between employer and worker met at the beginning of September in the Labour Exchange, St Anne Street. Six men received summonses for refusing to work overtime; they pleaded guilty and were each fined 20s (£1), to be deducted from their pay packets in four instalments.

During September, the Lord Mayor, who was chairman of the Liverpool Munitions of War Committee approached the Lambeth Road National Shell Factory general manager and explained a large amount of local engineering companies could only produce shells to a certain stage, having neither the required tools or skilled labour to complete the

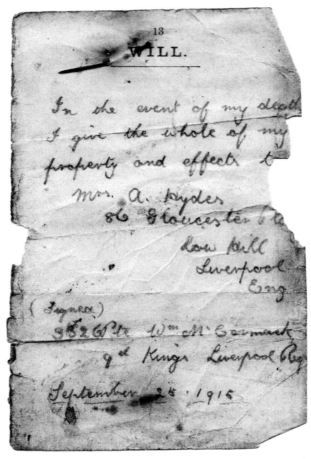

The army pay book will of Private William McCormack, 9/King's, dated 25 September 1915.

shells. In view of the work being in the national interest, work commenced at once on the contractor shells. It transpired some 300,000 shells required rectification, of which 75,000 were practically ruined and required careful attention to avoided being scrapped. The remaining 225,000 were not as bad, but had to be dealt with carefully. Each week, outside contractors delivered between 12,000 and 21,000 shells and by astute staffing arrangements the factory was able to complete the contractors' shells and still manufacture a considerable amount from start to finish. Early in October, the factory took on women workers; their numbers ultimately rose to the required 85 per cent.

There was a tangible reminder of the horrors of war when, on 9 October, in front of the partly constructed Cunard building, a *Lusitania* ambulance commemorating those who perished on the *Lusitania* was handed over to the BRCS. The Cunard directors and employees financed a pair of *Lusitania* ambulances, one of which was already employed at the front. The Bishop of Liverpool now dedicated the latest ambulance which bore the inscription: 'To the glory of god and in memory of 1,200 men, women and children passengers and crew of the *Lusitania* slain by the enemy on the high seas, May 7th 1915. This memorial is given by the directors, staffs and crews of the Cunard Steamship Company limited, in Europe and America.'

On 11 October Lord Derby was appointed Director-General of Recruiting and several days later launched the Group Scheme, it was unofficially known as the Derby Scheme, which aimed to induce men between the ages of 18 and 40 to attest their willingness to serve. On doing so, they received khaki armlets bearing the Royal Crown

The Group Scheme caused much controversy.

signifying they were awaiting their turn to be called up if required. The scheme was divided into forty-six groups, no man in these groups would be called up until he had reached 19 years of age, and single men would be called up first. The last day to join the scheme was originally 15 December 1915.

In Liverpool 600 older patriots were employed in the Dockers Battalion and the 5 battalions of the Liverpool Volunteer Regiment mustered 750 men. Over 550 members of the Liverpool regular police force had enlisted, and making up the shortfall were over 300 Special Constables, but a further hundred volunteers were required. The specials were expected to work a minimum of four hours, one night a week. Others devoted their spare time to fundraising efforts.

Unmarried.		Married.	
Age.	Group.	Age.	Group.
18–19¹	1	18–19¹	24
19–20	2	19–20	25
20–21	3	20–21	26
21–22	4	21–22	27
22–23	5	22–23	28
23–24	6	23–24	29
24–25	7	24–25	30
25–26	8	25–26	31
26–27	9	26–27	32
27–28	10	27–28	33
28–29	11	28–29	34
29–30	12	29–30	35
30–31	13	30–31	36
31–32	14	31–32	37
32–33	15	32–33	38
33–34	16	33–34	39
34–35	17	34–35	40
35–36	18	35–36	41
36–37	19	36–37	42
37–38	20	37–38	43
38–39	21	38–39	44
39–40	22	39–40	45
40–41	23	40–41	46

A bureaucratic nightmare of forty-six categories of men.

During the past twelve months, officials of the Flag Day Committee had raised £10,000 for various war relief causes. They now arranged a flag day to finance the local organisations which were already engaged in the task of despatching home comforts and bread to servicemen interned in German prisoner of war camps. As Christmas approached the Lord Mayor arranged a flag day for the provision of food and clothing for Lancashire and Cheshire men forced to spend Christmas in a German internment camp.

About 1,200 ladies were involved in the Flag Day, and collectors covered all parts of the city, including the docks and suburbs. At St George's Hall the sellers included Territorials and detachments of the 2nd, 4th and 5th (Aintree) Boy Scouts. The Flag Day raised £1,200.

The logistics of providing comforts for prisoners in other theatres of war was impractical. On 5 October an Anglo-French Salonika Force landed in Greece to fight the Bulgarians, in one of the most overlooked campaigns of the conflict. On the Western Front the Italians made little headway against the Austro-Hungarians and by early December British

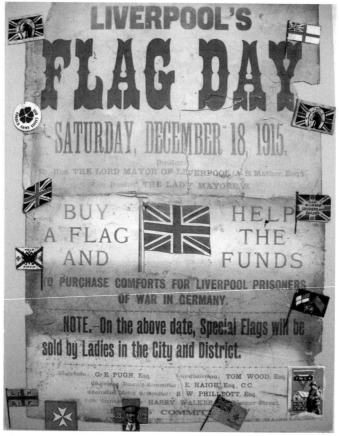

A patriotic red, white and blue Liverpool Flag Day poster for 18 December 1915.

forces were under siege at Kut-el-Amara in Mesopotamia (Iraq). The garrison surrendered on 29 April and 13,000 men were captured; over a third would die from sickness and neglect. And as Christmas approached the surreptitious evacuation of Gallipoli commenced thus drawing down the curtain on the debacle of the Dardanelles campaign. After a year of worldwide bloodletting, little, if anything had been achieved in the deepening conflict.

CHAPTER 4

1916
The Realisation

As the New Year dawned those reflecting on the previous year would have gained little consolation from the naval and military manoeuvres. The Western Front was frozen in aspic and the Royal Navy, colloquially referred to as John Bull's teeth, looked increasingly fallible. The realisation dawned that the British Empire was embroiled in a war of attrition from which a British victory could no longer be guaranteed. Against this faltering military backdrop, the home front had evolved into an ever more productive supplier of all manner of essential products ranging from knitted gloves to battle ships, but recruitment was in decline.

At the request of the Secretary of State for War, Lord Derby had agreed in October to undertake the task of recruiting the army. At the beginning of the year he reported that the National Registration details revealed more married men than bachelors had enlisted or attested and 1,029,231 single men shirked military service.

But, as Derby's Military Service Bill began to loom, men attested (signed up) under the Group Scheme and were assured single men would be called up first. After attestation, the majority of volunteers returned home to await their call-up papers when the Military Service Act of 27 January 1916 came into force.

Their compliance rankled with the Society of Friends (Quakers) and members of the Socialist Labour Party, who formed the No Conscription Fellowship and had successfully campaigned for a conscience clause in the 1916 Military Service Act. On moral and religious grounds the Conscientious Objectors (COs) refused to break the sixth commandment, 'Thou shalt not kill', whatever the circumstances.

The defiant men comprised three categories. Absolutists rejected any form of alternative war service. They refused to take up arms or participate in diverse civil employment encompassing building rifle ranges to sack making, for the end product could be used for coaling warships. Alternativists shunned weapons training and soldiering, but were willing to work in occupations not controlled by the army, such as agriculture. The 'non-combatants' accepted military service but only in a non-combatant role, and several thousand of this class served in the RAMC as medics or front-line stretcher-bearers. An early March 1916 Royal Warrant authorised the formation of the Non Combatant Corps for men who had been refused total exemption from military service. Dubbed the No Courage Corps by the press, the NCC were willing general labourers for any task except handling munitions.

Ultimately, over 16,000 men claimed the right of exemption from military service. More than 6,300 COs were court-martialled and

The COs depicted singing love songs to advancing Germans.

incarcerated, and of these over 800 spent more than 2 years in jail. In common with other prisoners, they endured hard labour, talking was forbidden, sometimes a bread and water diet and instances of brutality. The uncompromising regime led to seventy-three deaths, while others left prison physically broken or mentally ill. Decades later a variant of this press-gang descendant would force other generations to a stint of military service; British conscription was finally laid to rest in the 1960s.

At the height of the war those deliberately avoiding military service were treated with disdain by the majority of the population. Most families had someone serving in the forces defending King and Empire and uncooperatively the stay-at-home. Public scorn was both verbal and literary, with the following derisive verse appearing in a Cambridgeshire newspaper.

The Shirker's Alphabet

A's for the Army, where nothing could send him:
B's for our Best, who have died to defend him.
C is for his Conscience, so tender – and new;
D is the Duty it won't let him do.
E is for England, whose call he refuses;
F is for the Funk underneath his excuses.
G's for the German's whose hearts he's delighting;
H is his Home for which others are fighting.
I's his snug Income, without any tax;
J's the soft Job that he sticks to like wax.
K – well it's K [Kitchener] who will fetch him this year;
L is the Life he will lead then, I fear.
M's for his Motto – 'Number One First'.
N's for his Nickname – 'One of the worst'.
O's his Objection to go and get shot:
P's for his Pals, the Pacifist lot.
Q's for the Quibbles they cram in his brains;
R's the Religion he often profanes.
S is for the Shame that he brings on our race;
T's the Tribunal he tries to outface.
U is the Union of every true worker;

V is for Victory, spite of the shirker.
W's Women he'd let the Huns kill;
X the Ex-emption he's begging for still.
Y is a question – 'Why cannot we mend him?'
Z is for Zepps – and we'd thank one to end him.

The COs were reviled as shirkers at a time when stepping forward in droves were the ground-breaking female war workers, who often had relations serving in the army or navy. In January, the North Haymarket National Shell Factory, now working seven days a week, commenced employment of enthusiastic women machinists; in a condescending tone, it was recorded after four hours training on a single operation they became quite proficient in that operation. The women worked on a three-shift system of approximately eight hours duration, the more robust male workers worked a two-shift system of approximately twelve hours.

As an indication of the personnel involved, the North Haymarket canteen had seating for 600 diners who ate low-cost substantial meals. Possibly the installation of two sets of high-pressure heating systems necessitated the enclosure of the open eastern side of the market; the required materials were purchased from the old Exhibition Ground in Edge Lane. At about this time production faltered due to the arrival of new machinery provided by the Ministry of Munitions. Surprisingly, the machines lacked the special chucks, mandrills, boring rests, etc. required for shell production, and great difficulty was experienced in sourcing sufficient small tools to cope with the shell output.

NOTICE
ALL WORKERS
ON
MUNITIONS
WILL WORK
IN
SHIFTS
BY ORDER

"Well, I want to do my bit, but I draw the line at that !!"

A play on words of the modern style of dress – shifts.

There was however a boom in badge making. At the beginning of January the wearing of assorted drilling corps badges was discontinued in favour of the Central Association Proficiency badge.

The Liverpool Volunteer Guard commanded by J. Formby had grown considerably, as evidenced by the diversity of separate corps and company locations.

*Central Association
VTC badge.*

The Liverpool Tramways Volunteer Corps (Engineers), headquarters 21 Hatton Garden.
A Company Dingle and Garston district.
B Company Walton and Litherland district.
C Company Green Lane district.
D Company Smithdown Road district.

First Local Public Service Battalion, Commandant Ernest W.
  Pierce.
Second (North) Battalion, Commandant Major R. R. Daly
  Volunteer Decoration (VD).

Kirkdale VTC
Third (South) Battalion, right half, Commandant Lieutenant
Colonel W. Wainwright VD; left half, Commandant R. F.
  Daglish.

Fourth Battalion Liverpool Volunteer Reserve, Commandant
  Charles Stewart.
Athletes VTC Battalion, right half, Sub-Commandant R. G.
  Nicholson, headquarters Corn Exchange.
Home Defence VTC, left half, Sub-Commandant J. L. Murphy,
  headquarters 2 Shaw Street.

Fifth Battalion Liverpool Volunteer Reserve (National Volunteer
  Reserve), Commandant W. J. Fraser, headquarters Dingle Lane
  council schools.

Liverpool Volunteer Reserve (National Volunteer Reserve),
  Mechanical Transport Column, Commandant W. J. Fraser,
  headquarters North Haymarket, Cazeneau Street.

VTC members equipped for trench digging.

Second Battalion South-West Lancashire Volunteer Regiment,
 Commandant Lieutenant Colonel J. C. Eaton VD, headquarters
 Crosby Road North Council School, Waterloo.

The corps fulfilled a variety of duties and may have been involved
with the duty free bonded store opened by the Liverpool BRCS on
20 November. By mid-January 173,000 cigarettes and 230lb of tobacco
were supplied cheaply to local military hospitals. The Liverpool
Volunteer Guard also performed crowd control duties including the
ceremonial unveiling of the Liverpool Roll of Honour. On 20 January,
in Exchange Flags, the Lord Mayor drew aside the Union flag from
one of a pair of self-supporting heavy ornate dark timber frames
containing the Roll of Honour. The Roll went on permanent display in
the Town Hall entrance, where, on 11 May, the second Roll was
unveiled.

A few days after the first unveiling, the Mayor and Mayoress invited
500 wounded to the Town Hall ballroom, the hosts individually
welcoming each guest. They also presented the guests with a souvenir
brochure bearing the words: 'For your bravery, for your patriotism, for
your endurance, for all you have done for this country, the citizens of
Liverpool thank you most heartily'. They were entertained by Royal
Court Theatre artistes, including Little Tich, followed by tea.

Entertaining the wounded and fundraising became a national occupation. At the beginning of February, the shareholders of Liverpool Football Club agreed to provide a £570 ambulance to the BRCS, to be called the Liverpool Association Football Club Ambulance. On the same day, Goodison Park hosted a football match between the 22nd (Reserve) King's and the 1st Garrison Battalion of the Manchester Regiment. Both sides scored three goals, the winner being the BRCS, which received the match takings.

Attempts to cease Association Football games had failed, and much to the annoyance of the Jockey Club nearly all racecourses including Aintree were ordered to suspend racing. The War Office took over the Aintree course and consequently no races were held between 1916 and 1918. The Grand National became the War National and this was held at Gatwick racecourse, the site later being developed into Gatwick airport.

Mass passenger air travel was then unheard of, although airships were blazing a trail, in more ways than one. Until now the twenty-eight

Liverpool Town Hall.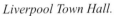

Zeppelin raids had concentrated on east-coast targets, but now Germany intended to show Britain they could penetrate the breadth of the country with impunity. On the night of 31 January, nine airships loaded with incendiary and high explosives soared into the air, and set a course for Liverpool, their objectives the flour mills and grain elevators on both banks of the Mersey. Adverse weather, navigational problems and mechanical difficulties resulted in the aircraft going off course. Kapitänleutnant Max Dietrich commanding *L21* was 70 miles off course when he mistook the lights of Derby for Manchester, and the featureless Shropshire and Welsh countryside for the Mersey. When Dietrich was north of Birmingham, owing to poor visibility, he mistook the lights of Tipton and Wednesbury for Birkenhead and Liverpool respectively. The airships were scattered across the Midlands when they disgorged their payload. There were 61 people killed and a further 100 injured.

The air raid embarrassed the government, for the dirigibles had again delivered their payload with impunity. Across Britain more stringent anti-aircraft measures were invoked under DORA regulations. In Liverpool and district, with effect from 5 February, all external public or private lighting viewed externally had to be extinguished, except where the Chief Police officer deemed it necessary for safety. The intensity of shop lighting was reduced, and tram lighting reduced to a level sufficient only for collecting fares. Households were advised to fit black-out window blinds and keep buckets of sand and water upstairs to extinguish incendiary bombs, and in the event of approaching aircraft, the electric and gas would be shut off. Persons contravening the regulation faced a court appearance and fine.

On the night of the aforementioned air raid, the 35th (Bantam) Division began to embark for France, and included in their number were the men of the 15th and 16th Cheshire. It would take time for the division to concentrate for units had disembarked at two ports. After having undergone a period of trench induction in a quiet sector, they advanced to the firing line.

The 15/Cheshire War Diary contains the stark entry: 'Gore, 28/2/16. Trenches. 1 man killed. 1 man wounded.' The deceased soldier was Private Weightman who prior to joining the Cheshire Bantams lived with his mother and younger brothers at 24 Whittier

Street off Smithdown Road. The senior Commanding Officer wrote to Alfred Bigland and his peers advising: 'Private Weightman of Liverpool was the first [Cheshire] Bantam to die for his country. We buried him in a little British cemetery [Windy Corner Cemetery, France] quite close to the firing line, and we put up a cross with his name and regiment on and a Cheshire cap badge on the top.' The undersized volunteer had made the ultimate sacrifice for his country as others stayed at home.

Thousands of voluntary clerical volunteers now applied themselves to implementing the compulsory call-up. The first summoned were single and childless widowers between the ages of 18 and 41 who had attested under the Derby Scheme. But the administrators' unfamiliarity with the Group Scheme resulted in March in the premature call-up of married men, instead of attested bachelors. Protests followed and as a consequence in May a revised Military Service Act was introduced. Regardless of this, the systematic calling up of married men would inevitably have caused great concern to their dependents in an era when the male was usually the primary wage earner. The introduction of conscription ended the chicken hunt and males from a wide demographic now faced an uncertain future.

Nonetheless, some 800 Liverpool dockers had enlisted. In mid-March, the Harrison Line attempted to introduce female porters at Toxteth Dock as replacements for the attested men; women also commenced working in the Leyland Line warehouses. Most dock workers refused to work alongside the women, but instead of going on strike they worked in alternative docks; the attempt to introduce women dock workers failed.

However, three soldiers mounted a successful action in April which resulted in a meeting with George V at Buckingham Palace. Private Vincent Howard of the Scots Guards resided at 72 Devon Street, off Stafford Street, Liverpool. When held captive in a German camp at Munster, Westphalia, Howard and two colleagues escaped on a dark night when snow was falling heavily. For three nights they travelled through mud and floods some 50 miles to the Dutch border, concealing themselves in ditches during the day. Private Howard: 'We were nearly done when we had to cross a railway line near Holland. We were spotted by a soldier who called out, then fired two shots at us. We ran for all we were worth and got away'.

Getting away with anything was contrary to the objectives of Liverpool police, for the newspapers were littered with reports of DORA transgressors who in keeping with the times received uncompromising sentences. Louisa Taylor of 11 Laith Street, whose husband was serving in France, was charged with supplying in her home intoxicating liquor to Lance Corporal Sullivan who was undergoing hospital treatment. Evidence was produced to show Sullivan had spent two nights at the prisoner's home. For the first offence Taylor received six weeks' imprisonment with hard labour, and a further fourteen days with hard labour was imposed for failing to get Sullivan to complete a lodgers' form in accordance with the Aliens Registration Act.

No such paperwork was required for the incapacitated at the overcrowded Seaforth Military Hospital. Annually over 5,000 patients passed through the hospital, and the difficulties the RAMC faced providing adequate nursing were almost insurmountable. In April, they requested assistance from Windy Knowe hospital where the Blundellsands VAD treated the Seaforth Hospital's acute medical cases.

Croxteth Hall became an officers' military hospital.

Croxteth Hall, Liverpool.

Under the supervision of the Windy Knowe commandant, four trained nurses were transferred and a new VAD was established for this work.

In May 1916, the mansion residence of the Earls of Sefton became a military hospital, but from July Croxteth Hall dealt exclusively with officer patients.

The social divide extended to a national Officer Families Fund, of which Liverpool was a contributor. For the corporation operated at least a score of funds for alleviating hardships locally and among the European Allies regardless of their social standing. One such scheme, the Roll of Honour Fund, existed to assist financially stricken families of deceased or gravely ill military personnel. For example, a husband of one applicant was an able-bodied seaman in the Royal Navy. He was discharged and sent to Rainhill Asylum, where he died. An application for the widow's pension was made in January and granted in October. During those anxious months the fund kept the widow and children. The fund had almost £38,000 in its coffers when Liverpool and Bootle held a Roll of Honour Week. During Flag Day, 500,000 collar lapel flags bearing a bunch of forget-me-knots on a blue background were sold. On 13 May, having generated over £4,000, the week of fundraising concluded with a military event on St George's Plateau.

On the first anniversary of the sinking of the *Lusitania* a new Liverpool monument was unveiled. Originally intended as a memorial to commemorate 122 engineers lost on the *Titanic*, it was dedicated to those who died at their place of duty on Liverpool steamers. The granite memorial became known as the memorial to all engine-room heroes. The memorial was paid for by international subscribers.

Liverpool schoolchildren were not to be outdone, for they had collected medicine bottles for the BRCS, which cleaned the bottles and then sold them to chemists. The initiative financed the 'Children's motor ambulance', and during a 24 May ceremony the vehicle was formally handed over, taking the city fleet to twenty-four.

The first cases of Conscientious Objectors appeared before the Liverpool Military Tribunal on 22 May. The appeals were presided over by a senior local councillor and Colonel Kyffin-Taylor represented the military. A 19-year-old Liverpool University electrical engineering student applied for absolute exemption on religious grounds. He was a member of the No Conscription Fellowship and believed war was futile and refused to take part in it. After careful

The 1916 memorial to engine-room heroes. The carved corner figures are Water, Sea, Earth and Fire.

consideration his exemption on conscientious grounds was refused.

The Bishop of Liverpool had been asked by a Conscientious Objector what his attitude to such objectors was and would he make it public; the reply appeared in the *Liverpool Courier*:

Dear Mr—

I have very decided opinions indeed about conscientious objectors to military service. I think that if they decline to fight for their country and are content to let others do it for them, their duty is to leave their own shores and take up residence in some other land where they will not be called upon to bear arms. Freedom of conscience does not mean believing anything you like, even though it is to the detriment of your neighbours, and declining to perform your duties as Christian men and citizens. This is certainly not the freedom of conscience for which our forefathers contended, and for which, if alive, they would have contended today.

Yours faithfully,

F. J. The Palace, Liverpool, 22 May 1916

The reasons for evading military service were diverse. In one case, three out of six brothers who were co-tenants of two farms in Melling appealed at the Liverpool Town Hall tribunal against the West Lancashire Tribunal's decision refusing them exemption. David, James and Stephen stated there were seven brothers altogether, the seventh, Robert being employed by the others. The two adjoining farms covered 137 acres and the appellants claimed they would be understaffed if the young men went into the army, Joseph was disabled, and Robert who was 32 years old was the only married man out of the seven. As all seven men were of military age and unattested and that four would be left to man the farm, the tribunal dismissed all three appeals.

On 2 June a well-built young clerk appeared before the Liverpool tribunal claiming absolute exemption. He stated he was unwilling to do anything directly or indirectly that would contribute to the

How I felt before the tribunal.

war. A member of the tribunal asked if the applicant would be willing to carry a rifle across to France for another man to use. 'Certainly not', was his reply. He was not granted an exemption.

The military tribunals continued throughout the war, and most of the appeals were similar to the above examples. Men who failed to register for military service or did not produce their registration cards appeared before a magistrate. The accused might serve a month in prison or be fined 40s to be deducted from their army pay.

Recruitment officers were now directed to re-assess previously rejected men, which led to claims of Derby Scheme rejects being bullied into the army. It was all a far cry from the vision of Lord Kitchener, who faced criticism over several issues

A frequently asked tribunal question.

including commissioning shrapnel shells instead of high explosives. The waning star embarked on a diplomatic mission to Russia, but on 5 June, off the Orkney coast, HMS *Hampshire* sailed into a minefield. Kitchener drowned together with 643 of the vessel's complement. The news staggered the public, and Liverpool flags flew at half-mast for Kitchener had been an honorary freeman of the city since 1902. Conspiracy theories abounded amid rumours Kitchener was alive and well. In September 1917, a Dale Street marine and general insurance broker underwrote Lloyds at a rate of £10,000 at 5 per cent against Kitchener's survival.

Shortly after the death of Kitchener the North Haymarket National Shell Factory received instructions to halt production of 18-pounder shells, and to turn the entire factory over to the production of the larger 4.5 and 6in shells. The existing machines required alterations and new tools and gauges were needed but the new shells were soon in

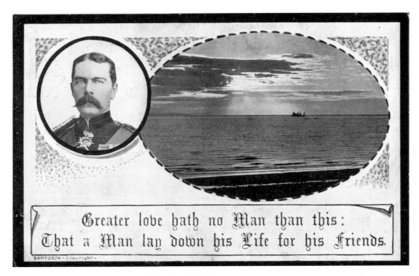

An in memoriam postcard of Lord Kitchener.

production. During the first year of its existence the factory produced the following shells:

18-pounder	245,672
4.5in	1,512
6in	5,024
TOTAL	252,208

By autumn, 85 per cent of the North Haymarket shell-manufacturing operations were carried out by female labour, while skilled men undertook the roles of supervision, tool making and maintenance. The old order had been swept aside; the conflagration was changing the social and political structure of Britain.

The previous June the Liverpool Munitions Committee had entered into discussions with the Munitions Ministry concerning the establishment of a Shell Forgings and Cartridge Case Factory, and also a National Filling Factory. The corporation's offer of a suitable site on Edge Lane was approved in September, together with authorisation to erect and equip the factory.

A munition worker's postcard.

The shell-forging factory, built on the former Liverpool Exhibition site, was designed for the production of 4.5 and 6in shell forgings. There were six 250-ton vertical hydraulic water presses installed and three gas-fired furnaces, each capable of heating thirty 6in billets an hour or the equivalent in 4.5in billets, and two 100 horsepower pumps provided the pressure necessary for working the presses. Production commenced in August 1916, and after a few months productivity was increased by the installation of a third set of pumps and modifications to the furnaces. Throughout the final quarter of 1916, the forges used 9,151 tons of steel and produced 78,670 castings of 4.5in diameter and 117,856 castings for 6in weapons. The following year the factory forged 32,894 tons of steel into shell castings.

A 45mm brooch issued to women munition workers.

The Cartridge Case Factory was furnished with a series of belt-driven gear presses for the production of 4.5in short howitzer cases, together with the necessary machines for finishing them. However, some machinery proved unreliable and required modification, and the lack of experienced workers further compounded production difficulties. Tellingly, the number of *good* cartridge cases produced in 1917 was 150,000. The following year output rose to 554,300 cartridge cases, the maximum weekly output being 25,000 cases; the factory closed shortly after the Armistice.

Acting on the suggestion of Lloyd George, the Liverpool Munitions Committee established a shell-filling factory at Bland Park Farm near Aintree railway station. The contractor, Bullen Brothers, commenced construction on 18 October 1915, and following the installation of American machinery the National Number Two Filling Factory began production in March 1916. The Liverpool Munitions Committee arranged for an alternative group of directors to manage the factory that went on to fill 17,577,429 cartridges of all sizes.

A lapel badge worn by volunteer war munition workmen.

In February, the Liverpool Munitions Committee had acquiesced to the Ministry of Munitions' request to erect a factory at Aintree for the production of the new explosive Amatol. The *Liverpool Courier* stated: 'the work accomplished at these factories, [National Filling Factory (No. 2) and the Amatol Factory] which were erected at Aintree, represent Liverpool's greatest contribution to the manufacture of munitions, and their output was so immense that it will be seen they must have formed a substantial proportion of the combined national production'. The explosives could only be safely manipulated between two critical temperatures, which required a hot-water heating system incorporating 63 miles of pipes with the surface area of the radiators equivalent to 4.25 acres. The Amatol Factory output comprised:

Shells filled (all sizes)	15,783,767
Exploders	12,277,112
Smoke bags	2,011,437
Smoke mixture (pounds)	2,209,122
Amatol (pounds)	46,977,597

A post-war edition of the *Liverpool Courier* recorded:

Aintree munition works occupied four square miles of land adjacent to the railway. The L&YRC laid ten miles of railway sidings for delivering the raw material and transporting the finished product. At the period of fiercest activity, four special trains were loaded and despatched to the ports of embarkation every day before noon. Each train consisted of fifty vans, and each van contained ten tons of ammunition, so that these four trains alone represented a daily transport of 2,000 tons, whilst immense supplies were got away during the afternoon and evening. From the time the Aintree munition works opened until Armistice Day, the tonnage carried from Aintree by the L&YRC alone was approximately 1,600,000 tons.

However, Armistice Day was just a distant dream, as all of Britain was alive with talk of the impending 'Big Push' on the Somme, although neither the timing nor location were to General Haig's liking. After a week-long bombardment of the German lines 100,000 British and French troops advanced across no-man's-land. The Germans took shelter in their deep dugouts until the shell-fire ceased. Then they hurriedly manned their trenches and the advancing waves of British infantry were mowed down by German machine-gun and rifle fire. On the 1 July 1916, the British suffered more casualties than the combined casualties of the Crimean War, the Boer War and the Korean War.

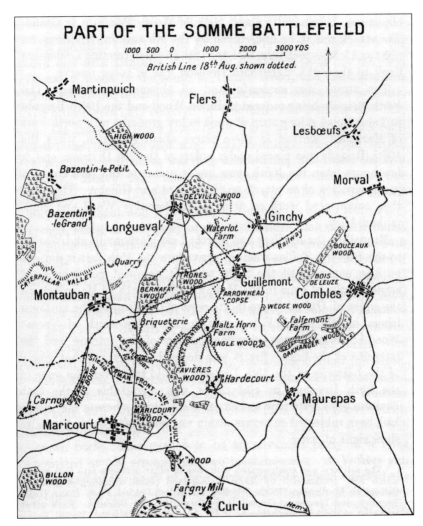

Map of the Somme battlefield.

The first day on the Somme was an unmitigated disaster, one of the few gains was the Manchester and Liverpool Pals' capture of Montauban. Private J. Warburton, a former employee of the Atlas Insurance Company now serving in the Liverpool Pals, wrote to his parents in Everton:

When we had our first chance of meeting the Germans, I thought them a very poor lot indeed. As soon as they saw us they started to run away. Those that were left in the trenches, as soon as they saw our boys enter, threw up their hands crying 'Merci, Kamerad'. Altogether we captured a goodly amount of prisoners. To look into some of their dugouts would surprise you. They had furniture; clocks, vases and chairs, and it put you in mind of a parlour. I am sorry to say that during the advance Alf Pearson (a mate) was killed. When we did go over our trench, we were met by a heavy fire from machine guns, but still our boys stuck to it.

The account tallies with the 18/KLR advance towards Glatz Trench, during which the battalion suffered 173 dead and several hundred more were wounded. It's probable the young soldier was 30804 John Edward Warburton, the son of Mr and Mrs Warburton of Wentworth Street, Everton. The 23-year-old was killed in action on 6 June 1918.

On the first day of the Somme 21,392 soldiers were killed or missing presumed killed, approximately 40,000 more were wounded and within a fortnight 2,000 wounded would arrive in Liverpool.

Ward A3, Mill Road Infirmary.

D Ward patients, 1st Western General Hospital, Fazakerley.

The urgency for hospital beds became evident at 6pm on 7 July when the manager of the Belmont Road Institution received notice that 100 wounded soldiers would arrive before midnight. The hospital had nine wards of civil patients mostly suffering from chronic infirmity and within a few hours they were transferred elsewhere. At about 11pm a hospital train arrived at Aintree and the ambulances delivered 200 patients to the hospital, which was twice the expected number, 'and all of them only roughly bandaged, and all bearing bitter traces of the ordeal through which they had passed'. Before the end of July Belmont Road Military Hospital housed 2,000 military patients, a number that was maintained for 3 years. The hospital later became a centre for the treatment of malaria and dysentery, and worked in conjunction with the Liverpool School of Tropical Medicine. There was also an infectious diseases block where 150 members of the Chinese Labour Corps were once confined suffering from mumps.

At the 1st Western General Hospital, Fazakerley wounded servicemen were also treated as out-patients, reported to a medical board or were kitted out with a new uniform. The men often experienced long delays and neither a rest area nor refreshments were available to make their wait more comfortable. Hospitals would 'telegraph for the attendance of relatives of patients who were in extremis'. Beyond paying the fare when necessary, no accommodation was provided for relatives. In the early days a hospitality committee made arrangements to board the distressed travellers with local residents until the patient succumbed to his injuries. This inadequacy continued until July 1915 when voluntary hospital workers secured the co-operation of the Women's War Service Bureau and the News and Recreation Rooms Committee of the Soldiers and Sailors Families' Association. Sufficient funds were collected to rent the nearby detached house 422 Longmore Lane as the Fazakerley Rest Rooms and Refreshment Rooms. Servicemen could now wait in comfort and purchase inexpensive good food and use the facilities for reading, writing or amusement. But this proved inadequate and the British Women's Temperance Association loaned a coffee stall, and for many months this was situated at the hospital gate until the hospital allowed the cart inside the spacious grounds.

As demand increased the Rest Rooms were converted to a hostel, and an adjacent shop served as a canteen. By mid-July 1916, precisely 241 relatives had received hospitality. But due to increasing casualties larger premises capable of accommodating seventeen relatives were rented at 1 Moor Park, Fazakerley; no charge was made for the food or accommodation, although donations were accepted.

These pioneering efforts in social war service would ultimately afford hospitality to 2,308 visitors. The coffee cart served refreshments to 317,968 customers and the hut supplied 49,367 men with refreshments.

Also providing invaluable service were the BRCS and St John's Ambulance which devised a novel method of fundraising. For four months Londoners visited the Knightsbridge Red Cross Active Service Exhibition until it relocated to Liverpool 'to allow people in the north to realise exactly the conditions under which are [sic] soldiers are living and fighting in France and Flanders'. On the second anniversary of the war, at the Ullet Road Recreation Ground, Sefton Park, the Countess of Derby opened the Active Service Exhibition, which was housed in two large marquees. Inside the first marquee the 3/Royal Welsh Fusiliers had constructed first and second line trenches linked by a communication trench. The marquee walls were lined with a gigantic panorama of the front drawn based on sketches made by the artist

The trenches at the Active Service Exhibition.

Dudley Hardy. The trenches were entered through a replica of a battered Flemish farmhouse, containing a machine-gun emplacement. There was also a sniper's post with sandbag defences, and a large number of periscopes were arranged to enable visitors to view the enemy lines, just as the British did at the front.

A second marquee was set apart for a display of captured battlefield relics, including machine-guns, portions of wrecked Zeppelins, shells, bombs and grenades, a working munition factory and a shell-damaged British 18-pounder. Eminent ladies staffed a fundraising gift shop, where a 10-guinea offer was made in a 16 July letter sent by Brigadier General Stanley expressing his appreciation of the City Pals battalions in the 'Big Push'. The women from 80 VAD helped at the exhibition, which opened from 11am to 9pm, the admission up to 5pm being 1*s* and from 5pm to 9pm 6*d*. Despite the cancellation of the bank holiday, the first-day attendance was three-and-a-half times greater than that in London; all profits went to the BRCS and the Order of St John. In mid-September, the aircraft of the late Zeppelin destroyer Lieutenant Warneford VC joined the exhibits.

At this time popular public places including cafes and theatres received the unwelcome attention of the police and military. Under the Military Service Act most men of military age were deemed to be enlisted and a nationwide hunt for those eluding the military began. The first local raid occurred on the evening of 27 August when the police barred all exits to Sefton Park and demanded the trapped men produce their medical exemption certificate or badge or paperwork relating to the Ministry of Munitions or other government departments. Those without paperwork but who had verified their identity were to go at the first opportunity to the recruiting office as non-compliance meant instant arrest.

By the beginning of September 300 Bootle men had fallen, and a score were being verified when a Roll of Honour ceremony took place in front of Bootle Town Hall. The 280 fallen comprised 9 officers and 271 others, with 63 belonging to the 7/KLR and a good portion of naval men. The Mayor officially unveiled the framed Roll of Honour before an audience of dignitaries, the families of the fallen, wounded soldiers, nurses, the Bootle VTC, Boy Scouts and a guard of honour provided by HMS *Eagle*.

But not all the population appreciated the self-sacrifice of British patriots. The pacifist movement had previously held meetings behind closed doors, but now the Women's International League staged evening gatherings in Holt Road, Kensington, another in Islington and a third on the corner of Beaumont Street. In Holt Road, a young lady bobbed up on a chair and addressed fifty people, but after a few sentences the crowd made their resentment known. Amid growing tension the police arrived and under their protection the peace delegates abandoned the meeting.

A few days later on 6 September the *Liverpool Courier* reported how the Liverpool Peace Push received a further set back during a meeting at the corner of Beaumont Street and Lodge Lane.

It had not been in progress very long before a placard bearing 'Remember Nurse Cavell and Captain Fryatt and the *Lusitania*', was hoisted. Mr H. Peel then declared his intention of making a protest against the peace propaganda. After reminding the audience of the German crimes and brutalities to prisoners, the peace party considered it advisable to depart, whereupon the following resolution was moved, seconded and carried by a large audience.

This meeting of Liverpool citizens denounces attempts made by the Fellowship of Reconciliation, the Union of Democratic Control, the No Conscription Fellowship, and kindred allied societies to obtain peace terms favourable to Germany. We declare no peace will be acceptable unless the districts invaded by the Germans are fully recompensed for the damage done, the authors of systematic and wholesale murders, thefts, rapes and inhumanities are adequately punished, and German militarism is completely crushed, and the nightmare of German aggression is banished forever.

We record our gratitude to all the brave soldiers and sailors who have made supreme sacrifices to protect our homes and families from German frightfulness, and to fulfil our national obligations and Christian duty to protect the small nations of Europe from oppression and slaughter.

It was a fine speech given by an orator equal to any eloquent member of parliament, which was now informed that after two years of warfare the retail price of principal food items had risen by 65 per cent. When questioned about the possibility of food rationing, the Prime Minister stated: 'I hope for voluntary avoidance of superfluous consumption it is the patriotic duty of all citizens'.

Others patriots were immortalised on 22 June when Lord Derby unveiled the Exchange Room War Memorial. And on Saturday, 9 September Prescot became one of the first towns to unveil its war memorial. This was originally sited at the corner of Church Street and Water Street. Due to the unavoidable absence of Lord Derby, the memorial was unveiled by Colonel Sir Henry Webb MP, commanding officer of the local barracks.

Prescot War Memorial, 9 September 1916.

Commemoration and amelioration were high in the public consciousness, and this was exemplified by the annual national fundraiser 'Our Day'. On 3 September the first airship to fall to British marksmanship crashed at Cuffley, Hertfordshire. The War Office

The packet contains a piece of wire 25mm by 5mm diameter.

donated the airship's wire framework to the BRCS, which sold it on 'Our Day'. In Liverpool pieces of the wire were fashioned into brooches or rings and sold at various prices up to ½ guinea (55p), while small pieces of the wire, in officially sealed envelopes, were offered for a minimum of 1s (5p). On 19 October, over a thousand Liverpool women and wounded men sold 750,000 'Our Day' lapel flags, and together with the wire sales the Flag Day raised £6,200 for treatment of the wounded.

To prevent discharged men in civilian clothes being castigated as cowards or presented with white feathers by indignant women the King approved the 12 September issue of the Silver War Badge. This was issued to officers and men of the British, Indian and Overseas Forces who had served at home or abroad since 4 August 1914, and who on account of age or physical infirmity arising from wounds or sickness caused by military service had, in the case of officers, retired or relinquished their commissions, or, in the case of men, been discharged from the army.

The incapacitated service personnel were brought home by a fleet of hospital ships including the 3,110-bed HMHS *Britannic*, the sister ship of the ill-fated *Titanic*. On 21 November the White Star *The 33mm Silver War Badge.*

liner was heading for Salonika. As *Britannic* steamed between the mainland of Greece and the Cyclades archipelago a mine blew a hole in the bow and ignited the coal bunkers. The nurses had opened all the ports to air the cabins prior to embarking the wounded, and as the bows of the ship dipped below the surface the water poured in sealing her fate and up to 1,500 personal abandoned ship.

Onboard were sixteen Sea Scouts, who served as lift attendants, ran messages and attended to the captain and officers, and ten of these boys were from Liverpool. When the ship was in its death throes, the Scouts attended to lifts and showed nurses to the lifeboats. Scouts E. Ireland and J. Price displayed great composure as they used megaphones to repeat the orders of the captain and chief officer. No more than six people were on board when the two boys slid down 50ft of rope into the water and swam to a raft. E. Ireland recalled:

> The vessel foundered in just under an hour, being struck at 8.12am and disappeared at 9.10am. At first the vessel went down slowly, but towards the end disappeared rapidly. Her propellers were out of the water, she heeled over on her side, and the last man to leave her, an aged man, who was dazed, was able to walk along her port side into the water.

The Liverpool Scouts were reunited with their families at Woodside station, Birkenhead on 5 December. The following March, at Liverpool Town Hall, the scouts were presented with certificates and compasses, and Patrol Scout Ireland in recognition of his great courage and endurance received the Cornwall badge. The award was inaugurated to commemorate the former Scout and Jutland hero John Travers Cornwall VC.

As the year drew to a close, the Lord Mayor unveiled the third part of the Liverpool Roll of Honour. Altogether the rolls commemorated 404 officers and 2,587 non-commissioned officers and men. But, the patriotism and valour of Britain's armed forces could yet be undermined for it looked increasingly like victory could be won or lost on the cornfields.

CHAPTER 5

1917
Seeing it Through

To some extent Britain tolerated the restrictions on civil liberty imposed by compulsory military service, but now the authorities were looking anxiously at food reserves and facing the prospect of introducing food rationing. Recently DORA had ordered hotels to restrict meals to three courses and it became illegal to feed wheat to animals and grain to game. Effective from 1 January, sugar was rationed to half a pound per head, while available. At the same time, millers were ordered to use standard flour instead of white, and extract from the wheat some 75 per cent of grain, and at the end of the month a further 5 per cent was demanded through extra milling or the addition of oats or barley. Following the introduction of the 'national loaf', white bread was a thing of the past, and the use of sugar or chocolate for the outside dressing of cakes was prohibited.

Inappropriate behaviour in munitions factories was also banned. A pre-Christmas jollification in an unidentified munitions establishment led to twenty young men making a New Year appearance before the Liverpool Munitions Court charged with not working diligently. They had worked normally until 2am but then sat around chatting and listening to a gramophone and drinking alcohol. They failed to return to work and 'showed a mutinous spirit as they walked around the workshop disturbing workers resulting in a loss of production'. The defendants were fined 15*s* each, to be deducted in three weekly instalments from their pay packets. In the same month, the North

Haymarket shell factory was ordered to cease Sunday production, which coincided with the alteration of the women's shift patterns in the factory to allow the men and women to share the same meal times. Generally, munitionettes worked a fifty-five-hour week for a decent weekly wage of £1s 8d, and when 500 Liverpool vacancies were advertised the positions were filled within a week.

Others opted for more genteel voluntary work. The War Dressings Supply Organisation utilised the Gallery of the Adelphi Hotel, while the Walker Art Gallery Red Cross workers produced roller bandages, night shirts, shirts and ward shoes with crochet soles for patients suffering with trench foot. Their efforts are now largely forgotten, including Mrs Arnold Rathbone whose vacated home 'Crofton' was established as a fifty-five-bed military hospital in January.

Far away from the serene hospital wards, the war reached a new level of barbarity on 1 February when the German government announced that it would 'henceforth tolerate no hospital ship' in defined areas and would contrary to the Geneva Convention treat hospital ships as legitimate targets. The neutral Americans were becoming increasingly fractious and following the German decision to conduct unrestricted submarine warfare, they severed diplomatic links with Germany. From mid-March, American merchant ships followed

Women making bandages for hospitals.

the Anglo-French lead and commenced fitting their merchant ships with stern-mounted defensive guns. In the House of Commons, the First Lord of the Admiralty reported in the first 18 days of the month 134 British, Allied and Neutral merchant ships were lost, and described the submarine menace as grave, and the problem still unresolved. Merchant ships damaged by torpedoes or mines regularly limped into port laden with precious foodstuffs. In Liverpool the grain from flooded cargo holds was unloaded and kiln dried for either human consumption, animal feed or in the case of damaged rice used to manufacture cordite.

The potato's lament.

As food shortages began to bite, prolonged bad weather and a shortfall in labour prevented coal reaching merchants. In Crown Street, hundreds of people of all classes attempted to get coal and one firm was forced to call in the police to restore order. There was also a potato famine as the military used three-quarters of all potatoes produced. Towards the end of February, Liverpool market had only 20 tons of potatoes compared to their usual 200 tons.

For certain males the food shortages would no longer pose a problem as in October the army age limit was raised to 41, and all fit army clerks were transferred to combatant roles. In February, the dragnet for men resulted in recruiting offices receiving instructions that all men aged between 18 and 22 inclusive, passed for General Service and employed in government establishments, or badged (munition) firms, should immediately be called up regardless of their occupation.

David Lloyd George, who was now prime minister, announced that due to shortages all non-essential imports were restricted or prohibited. Imported paper was reduced by half and foreign tea (except from the Indian colony), coffee and cocoa were banned. Food prices were fixed by the state to avoid speculation, and as a stimulant the government offered farmers guaranteed prices for their produce.

In mid-March, appeals were made to households to use vacant gardens for crops, utilise food waste, particularly fat and bones, all vegetables and paper and cardboard. In mid-March, the football fields at Sefton Park were ploughed up ready for wheat production. Liverpool clubs and restaurants agreed to potato-less days on Monday and Thursday, and the Town Hall caterers totally banned potatoes to help the poorer classes procure them.

Further pessimism would have been generated during March when the Windy Knowe Military Hospital transferred to the larger Beach Road Schools. The commandant was made acting matron in charge of nursing services and also managed a female staff of fifty workers. The future looked increasingly negative but some solace may have been gained on 6 April, when President Wilson received approval to declare war on Germany.

Later that month, a special committee appointed by Liverpool Corporation to invoke the Cultivation of Lands Orders reported it had arranged for 2,750 household allotments to be cultivated, amounting to approximately 218 acres. The corporation had also ploughed up some 223 acres, in addition to 526 acres which were previously under cultivation by the various corporation committees, so that there was a total of 967 acres of land (roughly 1½ square miles) provided by the corporation then under cultivation. For this the corporation supplied 2,500 tons of horse manure, and the United Alkali Company made available 30lb of super phosphates for each allotment. Potato crops were prioritised but owing to a shortage of seed potatoes the remaining land was planted with wheat, oats or other crops.

At the opposite end of the food chain Mr Bibby, of seed crushers and oil refiners' fame, attended the Military Appeal Tribunal in the hope of retaining 'called up' men. During the proceedings it was mentioned that due to a shortage of labour he employed forty Conscientious Objectors from Wakefield Jail. They were paid 8d a day, the firm housed them and they were subject to regulations including a night curfew. As a result of behavioural issues, the firm had returned about half to Wakefield, and Mr Bibby doubted if he would employ more as they were a cause of friction among his other employees.

Also facing incarceration where the eight defendants involved in the Liverpool recruiting scandal, 'a crime of conspiracy of a particularly sinister and mischievous character', the trial for which began on 20 April at the Liverpool Assizes. The case revolved around Captain Herbert Wilson, the former chief military substitution officer at Liverpool. During the re-organisation of the Liverpool recruiting department, irregularities were found in Wilson's paperwork, suggesting payments were being received for the avoidance of military service. This led to Wilson appearing in Liverpool Assizes along with five other bailed defendants. They were charged with conspiracy and of corruptly giving or receiving money for the purpose of evading the Military Service Act 1916. From the outset, Captain Wilson pleaded guilty, and at the end of the week-long trial the judge stated, 'It would be very difficult for me to express the grief I feel on seeing a man of your undoubted abilities, a man of your character and career in this position'. On sentencing consideration was made for the useful statements Wilson had made to the police; he received a prison sentence of one year and nine months.

The case, which was very complicated, involved seven other defendants including 60-year-old John Hughes, who owned fifty grocery stores in Liverpool, Bootle and Birkenhead, and employed a large number of men of military age. In the early part of 1916, there had been for some time an ongoing voluntary process of attestation, the men being enlisted in groups according to their age, and then being called up in consecutive groups. Hughes knew a large number of his staff had attested voluntarily, and that still more of his staff would come within the scope of the Military Service Act. In May 1916, Hughes paid a sum of £400 to Captain Wilson, who had it in his power to confer illegitimate advantages on him. By January 1917, Wilson had received instalments amounting to £875. He was also charged with making false statements under DORA. Throughout the proceedings Hughes proclaimed his innocence. On passing sentence the judge remarked: 'Your case is in some respects the worse of them all. You are a man in a good position, a man of considerable wealth . . . You have been found by the jury upon such evidence as I myself do not think they could rightly come to any other conclusion'. The judge imposed a sentence of twelve months' imprisonment and a £200 fine.

Another defendant was found not guilty. A drapery travelling salesman, he feigned heart and mental incapacity, but was in collusion with Wilson and pleaded guilty to a charge of making false statements.

He was discharged but ordered to join the army at once. The other four received sentences totalling thirty-three months.

They were detained at His Majesty's Pleasure when to assuage the gloom and doom, King V and Queen Mary made a morale-boosting tour of the northwest. After visiting North Wales and Chester, they toured the Cammell Laird shipyard, then went by car to Woodside and boarded the inspection vessel *Galatea*. After a short river trip, they landed in a Liverpool dock, where the King inspected certain portions, met merchant navy personnel, witnessed Khaki Dockers at work and passed through part of Bootle.

During the 15 May visit, the Queen visited two shell factories including the North Haymarket premises. During the conducted tour

The Queen visiting a Liverpool munitions factory crèche.

she showed a keen interest and conversed with the girls at their benches. After a visit to the second factory, the Queen entered the munition factory crèche. This was followed by a visit to 1st Western Military Hospital where over 2,000 wounded from hospitals across the district were in attendance. After a civic reception on St George's Plateau, the King presented gallantry medals to fourteen heroes and the royal party then left for Manchester.

As the food crisis heightened, George V signed a proclamation exhorting people to reduce their consumption of wheat and to practise the greatest economy and frugality in the use of all types of grain. Families were encouraged to cut back their consumption of bread by one-quarter and persons who kept horses were forbidden to feed equines oats or other grain unless they had a specific licence from the food controller. The directive was to be publicised on Empire Day, 24 May. At a crowded Exchange Flags, on the stroke of midday a trumpeter blew a fanfare preceding the Lord Mayor's reading of the proclamation, followed by a trumpet rendition of the National Anthem.

Meanwhile, in West Flanders, British engineers were adding the finishing touches to twenty tunnels (the Germans discovered one) burrowed towards Messines Ridge, south of Ypres. This natural

Eat less bread.

Exchange Flags.

stronghold, held by the Germans since 1914, dominated the British lines until 03.10 hours on 7 June, when nineteen mine heads crammed with 600 tons of explosives blasted the Germans off the ridge. The next day German counter-attacks were repulsed, subsequent counter-attacks decreased in intensity and by 14 June the British held the entire ridge and delivered a desperately needed boost to national morale, and removed a key obstacle to an impending British advance.

In the same month the Cunard Steamship Company arranged their third river trip of the season. No less than 400 wounded soldiers from 32 hospitals boarded the tender *Skirmisher* for a trip extending from Eastham to the Formby lightship. During the trip the Cunard concert party sang popular songs accompanied by the company orchestra. As the men left the tender they each received twenty cigarettes in a specially designed box, which had a combination picture of the Cunard building and the *Aquitania*.

Also in June the Select Vestry placed their Kirkdale home at the disposal of the Canadian government, which established a clearing hospital for soldiers returning to Canada. From September, the 5th Canadian General Hospital which had returned from Salonika took charge of the Kirkdale premises. The unit comprised 31 officers, 72 nurses and 203 other ranks and ministered to the patients until its closure on 26 November 1919.

But there was no end to the perennial problem of feeding the nation. In early July Liverpool Council established food kitchens at the South

End Day Industrial Schools, Northumberland Street and the Day Industrial School, Addison Street. The non-profit-making venture provided inexpensive meals including 1½*d* bowls of lentil soup or 4*d* bowls of Irish stew – also known as scouse. The customers provided their own crockery and took the food home.

On 17 July at St Peter's Church, Church Street, the Lady Mayoress unveiled a war shrine recording the names of forty men from the parish that had fallen. The framework of polished hardwood contained the scriptural passage 'Greater love hath no man than this' with a picture of the Saviour and the figure of a soldier on the battlefield who had made the supreme sacrifice featured below.

On the Western Front a fortnight-long British preliminary bombardment involving 2,000 field guns and 1,000 howitzers pulverised German defences across 18km of front in readiness for the Third Battle of Ypres. As an indication of Britain's ability to bite back, the barrage expended some 4.24 million shells. On 31 July, the infantry went 'over the top' to meet their destiny. Despite Haig's meticulous preparations to capture Belgian ports occupied by Germans, early successes foundered against in-depth German defences, and then

Renshaw Street war shrine. The poster on the far right advertises the Bootle Palladium. Note the two uniformed WAACs.

Britain and Flanders experienced the worst rainfall for forty-one years. The bombardments had destroyed the watercourses, flooded shell holes became death traps, streams burst their banks and swathes of ground became quagmires, paralysing the advance of British, Canadian and Australian troops. But they stoically pressed on in the mistaken belief that the Germans were on the verge of collapse.

On the home front, the incessant rain created difficulties for farmers bringing in the harvest. At about this time, the North Haymarket factory received instructions to halt manufacture of the loose-head type of shell and to switch production to shells from a new forging known as the bottled or solid forging. The factory was extended to accommodate new hydraulic pumps, presses and gas furnaces for production of the new type of shell. By 16 June 1917, the factory had manufactured the following shells:

18-pounder	245,672
4.5-pounder	72,423
6in	110,405
TOTAL	428,500

Munition work was not without danger. At the Litherland munition factory waste chemicals seeped into the sewage system and in late July caused the deaths of Arthur H. Carter, a surveyor, and Robert Forshaw, a council workman. Although the gases were unusually strong, the two descended the sewer in Bridge Road to clear an obstruction, but despite wearing respirators were overcome by gas. A third worker raised the alarm, but the rescuers were overcome by gas and hauled out. Smoke helmets were sent for, and a manhole 200yd away was opened. Two policemen descended and found the bodies jammed in a sewer junction owing to the flow of water. Attempts to revive them failed and the bodies were taken by ambulance to Stanley Hospital. The sewer gas turned red the buttons on the clothing of a bystander, an army captain, and the watch chains and coins of others turned a dark-green colour.

The incident was witnessed by army officer, author and poet Rupert Graves, who was gassed and wounded in France and now re-habilitating at the 3/RWF camp. In his autobiography *Good-bye to All That*, Graves wrote:

marching through the streets of Litherland on a battalion route march, I saw three workmen beside an open manhole, bending over a corpse which had just been hauled up from the sewer. His clothes were sodden and stinking; face and hands yellow. . . . My company did not pause in its march, and I had only a glimpse of the group, but it reminded me so strongly of France that, but for the band music, I should have fainted.

Prolonged exposure to the sulphuric acid in TNT can seriously damage the immune system and vital organs and lead to yellow discolouring of the skin. This explains why women who worked with it during the war were nicknamed canaries. They were constantly endangered because of the risk of explosion and taxed by excessively long workdays. In mid-August, as a result of nervous breakdowns

Women employees at the Cunard National Shell Factory, 1917.

Knowsley Hall.

among Liverpool and district women war workers, a six-ward convalescent home was established in a wing of Knowsley Hall, where the ladies could rest in ideal surroundings.

Also resting in mid-August were 8,000 men of the Mersey District Boilermakers Union, who contrary to the Munitions of War Act commenced an illegal strike relating to previous pay awards. Since the outbreak of war, the men had arbitrated pay increases totalling 15s a week. At a meeting between workers' representatives and the Ministry of Labour, it was made clear that the subject had been before other departments and the War Cabinet, and it was decided that whatever dislocation took place the department had to remain firm. The whole question of settling disputes during the war would be at stake if the Ministry of Labour had to concede to threats of strikes and rehear awards that had previously been given. As the strike was illegal, full protection against victimisation was offered to non-striking workers.

The front-line soldiers had nothing but contempt for strikers who appeared to be benefitting financially from the conflict:

> Sir, I have received a letter from a friend of mine, and he tells me the boilermakers in Birkenhead are on strike. I think myself that it is a shame to think that we have got to go and fight for them on one shilling a day and bully [corned beef] and biscuits while they are earning their three and four pounds a week. If I had my way with them, I should give them a spell in No Man's

Land, and let them be fed on bully and biscuits and drink water out of shell holes.

Sir, you can publish this letter in your paper if you think it is worth it. I am a native of Liverpool, but have worked in the shipyards of Birkenhead, and I think the men ought to be satisfied until this war is over. Of course, I daresay they will say they are fighting for us. Well I think those that are spared will be able to fight for themselves.

Yours truly, a wounded Tommy, 28 August 1917.

After negotiations in London, on 26 August, a mass meeting was convened at Liverpool Stadium. After a 4-hour debate, the 4,000 workers present agreed to return to work on condition a court of arbitration was immediately set up under the Munitions of War Act.

The shipbuilding and repair workers were a vital cog in the war machine, but the men and women of the mercantile marine were the unsung heroes of the First World War. A total of 14,661 perished in the service of their country and countless more survived the trauma and consequences of torpedo attacks. One such ordeal befell the reputedly Liverpool crew of the Ellerman-Wilson vessel *Hidalgo*. During a voyage from Manchester to Archangel with a general cargo and munitions the merchant ship was torpedoed and sunk by the German submarine *U28* at a position 120 miles northeast and ½ mile from Cape North. The following brief report by Captain F. R. Patten reached the hands of the Imperial Merchant Navy Guild.

28 August. 6.45am. Ship torpedoed without warning, and at once took a list to port. The port cutter was blown to pieces, wireless rendered useless, port lifeboat and starboard cutter were swamped, leaving one boat for all hands. Thirty-five out of thirty-seven were in the lifeboat, two men being drowned when the starboard cutter was swamped. The submarine then commenced shelling the ship, which sank stern first. Having seen the ship sink, we set sail making a southerly course for the land.

29 August. Strong N.E. wind, inclined to moderate gale with heavy confused sea.

30 August. Men suffering greatly from exposure. Second cook buried at 3am. At 5pm the donkeyman died.

31 August. Cook, second steward, two A B's [Ashworth and Grimes], also one fireman died. These bodies were kept in the boat.

1 September. Land was sighted southward. 8.20pm a landing was made at [censored]. We were given shelter by a fisherman named Severin Johansen, and everything possible was done for us.

The Guild was informed by their Hull representatives that several members of the crew had fingers and toes amputated owing to exposure, among them being the chief officer G. A. Hannah, whose three forefingers of the right hand were amputated.

Also imperilled on the cruel sea, were the Royal Navy who had a rare stroke of luck in late September when the German mine-laying submarine *UC44* struck a mine, and sank off the Waterford coast. On salvaging the vessel, the Admiralty recovered vital intelligence including how an average of twenty-five U-boats a month passed under cover of darkness over the English Channel anti-submarine nets. This reduced journey time to the Western Approaches by eight days in comparison to the North Sea route, saved fuel and extended by eight days the submarines patrol. However, Admiralty staff failed to deploy counter-measures. Finally, on 15 December the First Sea Lord lost his patience and ordered increased surface patrols and the barrage illuminated at night by searchlights; this had a significant impact on German submarine operations.

Meanwhile, on the Western Front the infantry stoically pressed on towards the Flanders village of Passchendaele (entered on 6 November by the Canadians). In modern times Field Marshal Sir Douglas Haig has unjustly faced criticism over the protracted campaign, and this stance is contrary to the following endorsement from David Lloyd George, issued by the War Office on 16 October 1917:

The War Cabinet desire to congratulate you and the troops under your command upon the achievements of the British armies in

Flanders in the great battle which has been raging since 31 July. Starting from positions in which every advantage rested with the enemy, and hampered and delayed from time to time by most unfavourable weather, you and your men have nevertheless continually driven the enemy back with such skill, courage and pertinacity and have commanded the grateful admiration of the British Empire, and filled the enemy with alarm.

I am personally glad to be the means of transmitting this message to you and to your gallant troops, and desire to take this opportunity of renewing my confidence in your leadership, and in the devotion of those whom you command.

The members of the Women's Army Auxiliary Corps (WAAC) were also looked on with increasing confidence. They were established in March 1917 for duties other than nursing. Some 6,000 members of the Women's Legion worked in army kitchens, camps and canteens or filled male roles as motor drivers, store women and telephone operators, etc. and it became obvious that a co-ordinating organisation was necessary. The WAAC arose from a combination of the Women's Legion and all other societies concerned with women's army work. The following year nearly 40,000 women had enrolled including some 7,000 who served in the rear areas of the Western Front, taking on roles so that men could be released for front-line duty, albeit on a reduced pay scale than their male counterparts. The women's section of the National Service scheme also comprised the Women's Land Army, the VAD and the Timber Section.

There were opportunities galore for women with a good standard of education. In September 1916, the Ministry of Munitions had selected Liverpool as a centre for training women for aircraft fuselage work. The work comprised light metal plate work, involving the accurate use of hand

A lot of fellows in the Army chew gum— but some prefer W.A.A.C.'s

Women's Auxiliary Army Corps.

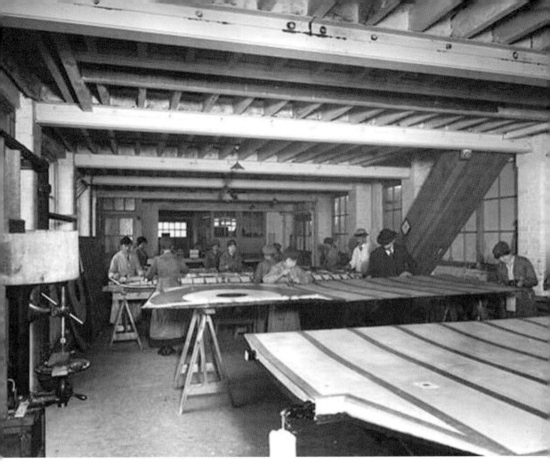

Women making aircraft wings in the James Troop workshop.

tools and measuring instruments and although it placed a fair demand on the physique, was not as heavy work as in the shell factories. A month's free training was provided at the Byrom Street Technical School, where the trainees worked an eight-hour day. The Ministry of Munitions sanctioned a maintenance allowance of 12s to the women who satisfied the conditions of training. On conclusion of their training they were allocated to aircraft factories throughout the country and received the wage of 22s and 6d a week.

With skilled workers almost on the doorstep, and in response to a shortage of military aircraft, the Liverpool Tramways Committee passed a resolution on 5 October, offering part of the Lambeth Road works to the Air Ministry and about 300 Avro main planes were manufactured. A further order for 200 main planes of the Sopwith Snipe type followed, which were under construction at the time of the Armistice.

In the quest to maintain air supremacy, under the powers of DORA 70 acres of Stag Farm, next to Aintree racecourse, were acquired as the site of National Aircraft Factory Number 3; the racecourse would serve as a runway. On 4 October construction began, with the contractor Trollop and Colls resolving building industry labour shortages by employing 3,000 Irish labourers who were unaffected by the Military Service Act. The factory opened the following March and was one of three managed by the Cunard Steamship Company. It was hoped 500 Bristol fighter aircraft would be produced, although by 1 October only 36 planes had been delivered and a dozen lacked engines. Production continued until March 1919, by which time 126 Bristol F2b fighter aircraft had been delivered.

Changes were also in the air at Highfield Military Hospital which by early November 1917 had treated approximately 4,000 seriously wounded men, and of these only 18 had died. In November a special section was devoted to jaw cases and facial disfigurements, owing to Alder Hey Hospital being unable to meet the demand for this specialist treatment.

Although Britain had unflinching determination to win the conflict, war weariness had inevitably set in, as illustrated in the following verse by H. Meredith, 17 November 1917:

When bacon and cheese drop to 9d a pound,
And there's enough sugar and tea to go around;
When old 'Turpentines' submarine crews are all drowned,
You can say the great war is over.

When Zeppelin air raids on London all cease,
When Turkey is roasted without the help of Greece,
And when all the Boches are praying for peace,
You can say that the great war is over.

When England and France stop the making of guns
When bakers start putting some currants in buns,
When Haig and our Tommies stop pushing the Huns,
You can say the great war is over.

When there's no excess profits no 'Government beer,'
When the controller assures us there is no profiteer,

When the sign 'Eat less bread' no more does appear,
You can say that the great war is over.

When from Belgium and Servia, the Germans are banned,
When the 'Rhine whine,' is heard in the Fatherland
When Haig, Maude and Beatty take a walk along the Strand,
You can say that the great war is over.

On 20 November the British commenced the Battle of Cambrai, an ambitious scheme launched on a 5-mile front (8km) aimed at piercing the Hindenburg Line and swiftly moving on to Cambrai. The battle, notable for the first mass deployment of 476 tanks, was initially highly successful, but the British were unable to maintain the momentum due to a shortage of infantry reserves, mechanical failure and the vulnerability of lumbering tanks to German short-range artillery. The advance was aborted on 3 December; both the British and Germans had sustained approximately 40,000 casualties.

At home, the tanks continued to enthral the public and the government capitalised on this fascination by assigning certain tanks to the promotion of War Bond investments. To this end, the tanks *130*

The Tank Bank 113 *'Julian'*.

and *113* were on display in Trafalgar Square for twelve days, and the tank banks amassed £3,423,264 in War Bond investments. On conclusion of the promotion, *113* made the railway journey from London to Edge Hill goods station, arriving on the evening of 9 December. Early next morning, tank *113*, christened 'Julian' and commanded by Lieutenant Lowe, clattered its way to St George's Plateau where the Lord Mayor made the inaugural War Bond contribution. At the end of Liverpool Tank Week £2,061,012 of War Bonds had been invested, setting a new record for a provincial tank bank campaign. With business concluded, 'Julian' led by the 2/Borders band crawled off to Edge Hill for a train to Manchester, the next city in the whistle-stop tour.

Also on tour was the successful play *The Better 'Ole*, by Captain Bruce Bairnsfather, which played for a fortnight at Olympia. Readers may be familiar with the wonderful character of Old Bill from postcards, books and chinaware. On the stage, Old Bill, acted by Ambrose Manning, came, as it were, fresh from the trenches, along with the mud and atmosphere of fears and hopes and examples of rugged humour which did so much to lighten the burden of those at the front as well as those at home.

On 12 December the Olympia staff, orchestra and various artistes freely gave their services for a benefit matinee performance in aid of the National Union of Journalists' Distressed Soldiers Fund. Ticket sales of the most successful NUJ matinee were boosted by souvenir programmes containing a sketch of Old Bill, specially drawn by Captain Bruce Bairnsfather. The original was presented to the Press Club, Liverpool as a joint gift of Captain Bairnsfather and the proprietors of the *Bystander*, a British weekly tabloid magazine.

Britain may have had the resolve to see the conflict through, but Russia had descended into revolution, and the new Bolshevik government signed an armistice on 16 December and began demobilisation. With the threat removed from the Eastern Front Austria and Germany were

Old Bill.

The 'Better 'ole' catchphrase was adapted for the NUJ matinee programme.

able to transfer men to the Italian and Western Fronts respectively.

As victory hung in the balance, for the warring nations there was little goodwill and peace on earth as the fourth wartime Christmas approached. The crew of the German mine-laying submarine *UC75* carried on their duties with murderous intent, laying mines off the Mersey estuary.

Alfred H. Read, *Pilot Boat Number 1.*

At about 3am on 28 December the pilot boat *Alfred H. Read* of the Lighthouse and Pilotage Authorities took up station when a loud explosion occurred holing the vessel amidships in the forward part of the engine room. Those in the engine room were either killed outright by the explosion or badly injured, although most of the forty-three men onboard were in their bunks. The pilot boat sank within two minutes, bows foremost and without having heeled over to one side or other. Five men managed to grab lifebelts and jump into the Mersey, and after a twenty-minute interval the small boats of another pilot boat responding to the explosion arrived and rescued three men.

The survivors, Alfred Davies (20, apprentice) of Denton Drive, Liscard, John R. Sweetman (19, apprentice) of 32 Alton Road, Tuebrook and Edward Beckett (18, Marconi Operator) of 61 Cecil Road, West Croydon, London were taken to hospital in Liverpool. Davies was later declared dead, taking the death toll to forty-one. The loss of the *Alfred H. Read* so close to home touched a nerve with the authorities who suppressed the media story. The 24 January 1918 edition of the *Liverpool Echo* reported: 'Following upon Mr Houston's questions in the House of Commons, we are now permitted by the Censor to publish the account of the sinking by mine in the mouth of the Mersey of a pilot boat on 28 December last.'

CHAPTER 6

1918
The Final Blows

In wartime the loss of a vessel in the Western Approaches was not unusual and men and ships were replaceable, but an army marched on its stomach and the food situation was still dire. Allotment mania was sweeping the country, and Liverpool was no exception. This was not surprising as 40 per cent of Liverpool men were country born and bred. The corporation had received a further 800 allotment applications, and now aimed to provide an allotment for every applicant. The lacrosse field and the cricket field in Sefton Park, which were ploughed up the previous year, became allotments. In addition it was intended to lay out allotments in Gardeners Drive, Newsham Park, Woolton, Gateacre, Wavertree Playground, Elm House Estate, Old Swan, Greenbank Estate and at Dingle.

Also in January, some 70 acres of the Bowring Estate were ploughed up and the farm field at Sefton Park, land in Wavertree Recreation Ground at Calderstones and the Walton Hall Estate were earmarked for growing food. The Ministry of Food encouraged a national cull of wild rabbits, as each provided approximately 2½lb of meat and was one less enemy for the crops and farmer; Boy Scouts were encouraged to assist in this process. The Ministry also advised bakers to use mashed or boiled potatoes in the standard 'National bread' to conserve cereal stocks.

Some United States Army 'dough boys', disembarking at Liverpool, required hospital treatment. Dr Edmund Muspratt of Liverpool offered his old residence Mossley House, situated in 7 acres, at the nominal rent of £10 a year to be used as a hospital. The premises became the first hospital for American soldiers established in Great Britain, and because of its location remained one of the most important. On 11 January Mossley Hill Military Hospital was formally opened as American Red Cross Hospital Number 4, under Major Udo J. Wile, formerly professor of surgery at the University of Michigan. But its 75 beds proved inadequate, so a pair of additional wards were erected to raise the capacity to 200 beds. A further enlargement became necessary and orders were received to extend facilities to accommodate 500 patients, and this required a complete re-arrangement of the plant with the construction work beginning in April.

The Americans were unwittingly in a war zone, for the previous September the area around Bolton was bombed. In late January the Chief Constable of Lancashire reminded Lancastrians of the air-raid warning:

A siren will give three blasts of fifteen-second duration with a few seconds interval, and one long blast of one-minute, the signal will be repeated after a lapse of two-minutes. Take to cellars or basements, turn gas off at the meter, and keep clear of windows and doors. Close windows to keep out noxious gases

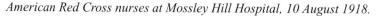
American Red Cross nurses at Mossley Hill Hospital, 10 August 1918.

from shells or bombs. The all-clear signal will be a siren blast of one minute followed by a short blast.

It was a timely reminder for on a dark and overcast 12 April night, Zeppelin *L61* flew over the Mersey and the blacked-out city and homed in on the light emanating from the blast furnaces of the Wigan Coal and Iron Company. People were unaware an air raid was in progress until seventeen bombs fell around Wigan, killing seven people and injuring twelve more; it was the last effective airship raid of the war.

The RAF had now perfected the art of airship destruction aided by the invention of a special bullet. Shell technology was also developing, and in February the North Haymarket Shell Factory invented a new adaptor or nose bush for shells with doubtful screw threads and this improvement was sent on to the Ministry of Munitions. About a month afterwards the design was made use of in shell factories throughout the country. About this time, the factory received orders to convert all machines engaged in 4.5in shell production over to the manufacture of 6in shells. And by June, all shell manufacture was carried out by women workers supervised by skilled men; the factory then employed 1,727 workers, of whom 1,360 were women.

Liverpool munition workers pose for the camera,
22 June 1918.

At the expense of the war effort industrial unrest continued, but as DORA outlawed strikes 'working to rule' became a means of obtaining improved working and living conditions. The rights of former servicemen and women were voiced by the organisation Comrades of the Great War, and on 1 February the first Liverpool branch opened at 38 Church Street. They merged with three like-minded associations on 15 May 1921 to form the British Legion.

A blue and gold enamel Comrades of the Great War lapel badge.

Huge numbers of American troops reached Liverpool on a variety of troopships, the most recognisable being the 950ft-long (289.6m) USS *Leviathan*, the former Hamburg–America Line *Vaterland*. This was seized in 1917, when the United States declared war on Germany. It was then fitted with eight 6in guns, a pair of 1-pounders and a pair of machine-guns. In December 1917 the troopship brought its first consignment of 14,000 troops to Liverpool, however due to repairs it was not until February that it returned to America. In March *Leviathan* again 'trooped' to Liverpool followed by another spell in dry-dock during which it was painted in the British dazzle camouflage scheme.

USS Leviathan *in the Gladstone Dry Dock, Liverpool.*

The Atlantic crossing generally took twelve days owing to the zigzag course taken to baffle U-boats. On reaching Britain the troops had a brief sojourn in a rest camp. The Liverpool arrivals marched 5 miles to the city outskirts where Springfield Park, Knotty Ash had been given over to military use. The former park had the advantage of being situated at the rear of Alder Hey Military Hospital, and 200yd from a main-line railway station. At first the troops were housed in an 'oasis of tents', but these were later replaced with timber huts.

The troops were also joined by members of the American Red Cross and American YMCA who no doubt provided copious amounts of American consumables. This was in contrast to local inhabitants who were informed by the Liverpool Local Food Control Committee that rationing of tea, butter or margarine would be introduced on 25 February. Householders had to apply between 4 and 8 February at one of seventy schools where they were aided in completing the ration card paperwork. Applications were refused if the householder failed to produce their sugar ration papers.

VERY LITTLE MEAT FOR A LARGE PLATE

RESTRICTIONS

Meat restrictions.

Retailers could only serve customers registered with their business. Meat rationing was inaugurated on 8 April. The four mandatory categories in the ration books were: Sugar retailer; Fats retailer; Butcher; and Bacon, but these, if available, could generally be purchased during a single visit to the local grocer.

At Liverpool's expanding communal kitchens (now a national movement) a family of two adults and two children could buy a meal of potatoes and gravy for 6*d*, but if the adults required meat, the price rose to 9*d*. The Northumberland Street kitchen also acted as a distribution centre from which food was taken by motor car to the following branches: 105 Kirkdale Road, 35 Netherfield Road, 28 Scotland Road, 254 Faulkner Street, 184 Park Road, 214 West Derby Road, 76 Earle Road and 371 Prescot Road, Old Swan. The latter three branches were experimental in the hope that 'better class residents might lose their prejudices when they realize the benefits of patronizing the kitchens'. In February, Miss Margaret E. Lamb donated £100 to the Mayor of Bootle for a communal kitchen, and others soon followed in the borough. The significance of these kitchens when the mortality rate of poor children was one in four should not be underestimated.

Neither should the interference in military matters of Lloyd George, who with one eye on home-front productivity and the other on servicemen casualties, had, for some time, been restricting the flow of men to France. Haig's divisions were now under strength; this led to Western Front brigades being reduced from twelve battalions to nine. Within the 30th Division, 89 Brigade shed three battalions, one from each brigade. Consequently, on 9 February the 20/KLR (4th Pals) were absorbed into the remaining Liverpool Pals battalions. Several second-line territorial battalions of the forty-five-battalion-strong Liverpool Regiment shared the same fate. The end result was Haig's force had diminished during a period when they were holding a much extended battle front and Germany was transferring seventy divisions from the collapsed Eastern Front.

A certificate presented to the family of Private Joseph Keating, 2/1 Oxford and Buckingham Light Infantry who died on 2 April 1917. His mother resided at 57 Menzies Street, Dingle.

As Germany prepared for an offensive, on 24 February Civic Remembrance Day was held and the sixth and seventh Liverpool Rolls of Honour were unveiled at Exchange Flags. The square was situated in the financial heartland of the city, the institutions of which were about to respond to the government's country-wide appeal for a further £100,000,000 invested in War Savings Certificates or National War Bonds. Business Men's Commercial Week commenced on 4 March, and cities and towns were invited to target a figure equivalent to the cost of a dreadnought battleship, battle cruiser, destroyer or an aeroplane. Ambitious Liverpool set a target of £2,500,000, equivalent to the cost of a super-dreadnought.

The focal point of the campaign was a 'highly creditable piece of work by the Tramways Committee', which outwardly modified a tram so it resembled a tank. This tram tank bank toured the area, and at selected locations speeches were made from the tram's open-top deck while post office officials sold bonds to the audience, and a large model of a super-dreadnought was displayed outside the Town Hall. After a week over £13,013,746 was raised, which put Liverpool at the head of the provincial cities in the matter of War Bond investments; in comparison Bootle raised £120,000.

The government had in October 1916 established a steering committee to create a commemorative medallion for the relatives of the fallen. By the following August, the committee had organised a competition to design this, with prizes totalling £500 for the winning entries. The design criteria for either a circular 4½in or 5³/₅in rectangular bronze plaque was published in the 13 August edition of *The Times*. An essential feature was to be the words 'He died for Freedom and Honour' and a space for the name of the deceased serviceman. For impartiality each entry had to be submitted under a pseudonym. The competition closed on the final day of 1917.

On 20 March, *The Times* announced numerous winning and highly commended entries, the overall winner 'Pyramus' receiving £250. The recipient was Liverpool-born Edwin Carter Preston, one of the first members of the Sandon Studios Society, Liberty Building, School Lane, Liverpool. He studied sculpture at Liverpool University of Applied Art but later devoted himself to painting, and was well known in Liverpool and London. His first success had been the previous year when he had contributed to a London exhibition of medallic art and received a first prize of £60 for the best set of struck medals. He also designed the medallion the Merchant Navy Guild presented to the 'six before breakfast' Victory Cross recipients who landed from the *River Clyde* on Gallipoli beach.

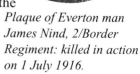

The *Liverpool Courier* considered Edwin Carter Preston's design effective because of its simplicity and direct expression. The medallion depicts Britannia crowning the name of a fallen hero. There is the figure of the British lion standing on the plinth, and figures of dolphins symbolic of Britannia as mistress of the seas. The British lion figure is also brought out in Britannia's helmet, while the exergue portion of the medallion

Plaque of Everton man James Nind, 2/Border Regiment: killed in action on 1 July 1916.

represents the lion overcoming the German eagle. The designer's initials ECP appear above the lion's front foot.

A parchment scroll giving the deceased's name and unit accompanied each 120mm-diameter memorial plaque, of which 1,355,000 'He died' and over 600 'She died' were issued.

This foresight was commendable, but first the nation had a war to win. Expectations were high that the great untapped human reservoir of keen but inexperienced United States of America troops disembarking at Allied ports would restore numerical superiority before Germany completed the transfer of troops from east to west battlefronts. But Germany was one step ahead for preordained plans had been gathering dust in German headquarters for some time; one such plan code named Operation Michael was adapted for a spring offensive. In the meantime, British strategy changed from offensive to defensive, confidently believing they could repulse any attempted German breakthrough. The distant Royal Navy blockade continued to exert an ever tightening stranglehold on German imports, leading to civil unrest among the malnourished civilian population.

Meanwhile, General Ludendorff finalised plans for a major offensive between St Quentin on the Somme and the Arras sector, a battle front of almost 50 miles. The main blows would fall on the Anglo-French army boundary and inevitably create maximum confusion, after breaching the Allied line. The British would attempt to defend the Channel ports and the French would fall back on Paris allowing German troops to head north and sweep the weakened British force into the sea, and France would then seek an armistice.

On 21 March after a 5-hour bombardment by 6,000 artillery pieces, General Erich Ludendorff launched Operation Michael. The troops using new military Blitzkrieg tactics crushed the thinly held Allied line. The British Fifth Army withdrew, in the process abandoning the Somme battlefields, but focusing their resources on the route to the Channel ports and the railhead at Amiens. Stiffening resistance and the rapid pace of the German advance prevented their replenishment of supplies and ammunition, and the momentum of the advance lost inertia, the crisis briefly abated. The British had suffered 178,000 casualties, the French 92,000 but the Germans incurred 239,000 casualties. The Germans had penetrated 40 miles (64km) on the Somme, but not achieved the desired result. On 5 April Ludendorff called off the offensive and launched an attack against the British on the banks of the River Lys. Again they made sweeping gains, and seven days later Haig issued his 'backs to the wall' rallying call and British resistance hardened.

In the face of this almost overwhelming crisis the munition factories

The first 6 and 8in shells made in the country by women workers at the Cunard munitions factory.

intensified their production by working additional hours including bank holidays. Armament works were now routinely checked for males carrying out work that could be done by females. The military dispensation for male war production workers was reviewed, and by mid-1918 this policy yielded a further 100,000 conscripts. The quest for men expanded its parameters in April when a Military Service Act amendment extended compulsory military service to 51-year-olds. Only the medically fit were accepted, although they were not intended for the front line and instead exchanged positions with younger men who were then transferred for front-line service. And, in May, regardless of their occupation any men born 1898 and 1899 were called up. Liverpool and district had between 80,000 and 90,000 men between 42 and 52 years of age already doing valuable war service, including Mr Galbraith, the manager of the Cunard Shell Factory, Bootle.

A 2 April 1918 letter of appreciation to Mr Galbraith.

The Cunard Factory management. Alexander Galbraith is seated centre front with his brother Fergus Galbraith, the works manager, next to him, second left.

The Cunard Shell Factory produced:

4.5in shells	201,426
6in shells	175,391
8in shells	33,900
TOTAL	410,717

In April 1918, at Springfield Park, American Camp Hospital Number 40 was established, and included several marquees of 150 bed capacity dedicated to the treatment of contagious diseases. Between 27 May and 6 June hospital Unit Q treated the patients, and thereafter Unit W took over. On 10 August a contract was signed for the construction of a permanent 500-bed hospital of traditional brick and concrete construction. This had two separate central heated buildings, a general section and a contagious diseases wing connected by a canopied walkway. Due to a shortage of labour and numerous strikes only parts of the hospital were operational by December. During its existence the hospital treated 3,909 medical and 901 surgical cases.

New evidence of British resilience was about to be driven home with a vengeance. The Wallasey Corporation ferries *Iris* and *Daffodil* (known as *Daffodil IV* during Royal Navy service) were powerful and easily manoeuvrable and each had capacity for 1,600 passengers; both ferries were requisitioned by the Admiralty. On 23 April, St George's Day, they played a key role in a combined naval and Royal Marine amphibious assault against the fortified Zeebrugge harbour wall, known as the Mole. During the height of the land assault, three block ships, *Thetis*, *Intrepid* and *Iphigenia*, slipped into the shell-swept Zeebrugge harbour and scuttled themselves across the channel to prevent U-boats from leaving the harbour. The gallantry displayed throughout the combined operation was recognised by the award of eight Victoria Crosses.

The scuttling of block ships in the harbour channels of Ostende and Zeebrugge humiliated the German fleet and implanted the grain of doubt that led to mutinies at Kiel, a pre-cursor to the surrender of the German navy.

The Admiralty played their morale-boosting trump card for all it was worth, and the patched up ferries were made available for public inspection at Falmouth and Portsmouth, with the modest admission fee being donated to appropriate naval charities.

On 1 April the Royal Naval Air Service merged with the Royal Flying Corps and formed the Royal Air Force. The following month, Liverpool Volunteer Flying Corps was inaugurated. This corps, the first

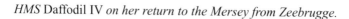

HMS Daffodil IV *on her return to the Mersey from Zeebrugge.*

in the country, was open to youths under military age, with the object of providing sufficient practical and theoretical knowledge of aviation to save a good deal of service time if the 18-year-old joined the RAF. Some 300 youths enrolled, and while the corps lacked an aircraft, lectures were given at the Bear's Paw, 53 Lord Street.

Those attending the meetings might have been inconvenienced by the reduction in the frequency of public transport. A shortage of miners and high demand for coal in Britain and Allied countries with coalfields occupied by Germany brought about coal restrictions. On 5 May, the Mersey Electric Railway were compelled to reduce their fuel consumption by 15 per cent, leading to a reduction in services. The tram cars finished thirty minutes earlier, although more stringent cuts were avoided because of the travel needs of munition workers.

Women disinclined to work in factories may have been interested in a recruiting drive for 30,000 Women's Land Army recruits organised by the Board of Agricultural Food Production, which resulted in a procession through the principal streets of Liverpool on 11 May. The pageant of women's war-time labour was led by 300 farm girls, in smocks, breeches and leggings, lady post office employees and women tram conductors, etc., and several bands. Farm carts decorated with produce and farm implements displayed banners of 'Britain must be fed', and 'Men in the field, women on the land'. The procession halted in Lime Street where the Mayor inaugurated the month's rally by addressing the crowds, and about 300 women gave in their names.

The army were now demanding more names to offset the battlefield casualties, as replacing them was becoming increasingly difficult. Sir Aukland Geddes, director of National Service, circulated a letter to local authorities increasing pressure on military tribunals to produce more recruits.

At the present critical stage of the war even greater efforts and sacrifices than those already made are necessary on the part of all classes of the community. The demand for men in the higher medical grades or categories is insistent, and must be met at once if the national forces are to be maintained in adequate strength. No fit man of fighting age should now receive exemption on occupation grounds unless he is engaged on work directly important to the prosecution of the war. There is a general paramount necessity that an increased flow of fit men should be obtained without delay to furnish his Majesty's Forces the support which is essential.

Curtailing the U-boats was also essential. After being on public display in Falmouth and Portsmouth, at 6pm on 17 May the two shell-battered Zeebrugge raid ferries, *Iris* and *Daffodil*, returned to the Mersey and anchored off New Brighton. The next day there was a mid-river civic inspection by local dignitaries. Later in the day the boats were taken into Canning Dock, Liverpool where they went on public display from Sunday until Tuesday evening. Over 10,000 visitors toured the boats, the admission fee proceeds, including souvenir programmes and picture postcards of the scarred ferries, totalled £1,380. Of this, £500 provided an *Iris* and *Daffodil* bed at Victoria Central Hospital (VCH); the balance went to naval charities and the Red Cross. Weeks later, in recognition of their role in this gallant raid, George V granted both ferries the prefix Royal, a distinction proudly borne by the current *Royal Iris* and *Royal Daffodil*.

HMS Iris. *The Liver building is visible due to the destroyed port wheel house.*

Flowers of a different kind were now requested for American Expeditionary Force members buried in Kirkdale Cemetery (most would later be repatriated). The short service arranged under the auspices of the American Red Cross and American YMCA was held on 30 May, American Decoration Day (now Memorial Day). A concerted attempt was being made to generate American goodwill, and on the same day, Liverpool linked with the American National Day of Prayer in fulfilment of President Wilson's call for all faiths and creeds in the Allied nations to pray for an Allied victory. Over 15,000 people attended a thirty-minute united Intercession Service held on Exchange Flags – perhaps their prayers were answered.

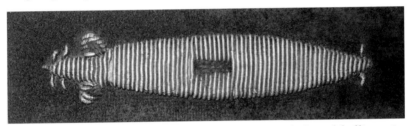

During mid-June, the Board of Trade awarded a cloth and bullion wire torpedo badge to masters and seamen who served on a merchant or fishing vessel sunk by torpedo or mine and afterwards engaged on another vessel.

The next day there was no such divine intervention for the patients of the Étaples district military hospitals who were singled out by German aircraft dropping 200 bombs. The Liverpool Merchants' Hospital was unscathed but the adjoining Number 51 hospital was hit several times with the buildings and occupants destroyed. The hospital committee received the following letter signed by twenty-nine officer patients:

We, the under mentioned officers, now patients in the Liverpool Merchant's Mobile Hospital, wish to place on record our unbounded admiration and appreciation of the most gallant behaviour and devotion to duty displayed by the staff of the hospital, under the able command and supervision of Lieutenant Colonel Nathan Raw C.M.G., in the air raids of the enemy during the past two weeks. [Adjoining army camps were bombed.] Under the most trying and difficult conditions caused by the heavy bombing, every possible care and attention was given for the comfort and protection of the wounded, and in this respect we would beg to offer our heart-felt gratitude to the matron, Miss Wilson, and to express our pride at the coolness and pluck displayed by our countrywomen.

The War Office decided to relocate all but two of the hospitals and the Liverpool Merchants' Hospital went to Deauville. 'Following the aerial bombardment of the hospital from 19 to 31 May the personnel, with certain exceptions were despatched to England on 4 June, as several of them were suffering acutely from the effects of the raids'. The staff returned to France between 19 and 20 July and worked in alternative military hospitals until 2 October, when they took possession of the relocated hospital and admitted in a single day 300 patients. The facility had the distinction of being the only military hospital which had been designed, built, equipped, staffed, managed and financed entirely by the citizens of a particular city. When the hospital closed as a result of the Armistice 19,172 patients had passed through the wards.

Another medic performing valuable service was the doctor Major John Utting RAMC, who became the Liverpool Lord Mayor in October. Unusually, the War Office allowed him to retain the rank of major and wear his khaki uniform throughout his year of office. He was under constant pressure for the procurement of funds for worthy causes, particularly from those agencies forwarding supplies including bread to prisoners of war. The large number of British troops captured in the spring offensive added to the financial burden. Utting launched an appeal for a million shillings and also wrote to the leaders of local political parties requesting assistance. In response, the Liverpool Workingmen's Conservative Association organised a grand raffle or tombola, with tickets priced at 2s 6d each and the first prize was £1 a week for life. Over 500,000 tickets were sold; the net proceeds raised for the Prisoner of War Fund amounted to £61,296. The grand draw took place in a packed St George's Hall on 30 September, the first prize going to Mrs Elizabeth Robinson of 16 Burnley Road, Brownside, Burnley. Second prize was a baby grand piano and there were dozens of other prizes including 2 tons of coal and War Bonds of varying denominations.

Also seeking funds were the YMCA who had lost 150 amenity huts and £150,000 worth of stores and equipment during the German advance. When National YMCA War Week started in late June, the Lord Mayor of Liverpool launched the Hut Fund with the intention of raising £50,000. A flag day and other contributions were boosted by Mr E. Carter Preston who charged visitors 6*d* admission to view his Rushworth Hall exhibition of paintings, polychrome models, drawings and the cast of the national bronze plaque. Overall the first week's donations were disappointing so the Mayor extended the appeal by a further week. The highlight of the second week was a mile-long procession of forty tableaux reflecting YMCA work, including an 'Our Wounded' float by the Seaforth VAD, a Bairnsfather 'Better 'Ole'

Our Lord (Military-Medical-Major) Mayor.

Lord Mayor Utting.

representation and a simulated Kaiser at which the public were invited to throw silver rather than mud. The city raised almost £62,500 and this placed Liverpool at the top of all the cities in the kingdom.

Heading towards the United Kingdom was a twelve-ship convoy from New Jersey. The Atlantic crossing took twelve days due to the zigzag course taken to baffle U-boats. On board three of the troopships were the 358th Infantry, a component of the 90th American Division, and they reached Liverpool late in the afternoon of 1 July to be greeted by thousands of wildly cheering people. The next day the 358th Infantry Regiment disembarked and marched to Springfield Park rest camp, one of the soldiers remarking 'this must be an English man's idea of a joke'.

At the request of Liverpool's Lord Mayor, the regiment remained longer than usual. On 4 July, the regiment marched from Knotty Ash through

YMCA Hut Fund lapel flag.

American infantry outside the Lybro workwear factory, Mount Vernon Green, Edge Hill, Independence Day, 1918.

the streets of the city in honour of American Independence Day. This was a unique honour as it was the first time American troops had ever marched through an English city commemorating independence from British rule. An estimated 50,000 spectators had gathered in Lime Street and around St George's Hall where the troops were reviewed by General Sir William Pitcairn the General Officer Commanding Western Command. A band played the 'Star-spangled Banner', after which each soldier was presented with the following message from King George V:

> Soldiers of the United States, the people of the British Isles welcome you on your way to take your stand beside the armies of many nations now fighting in the Old World the great battle for human freedom. The Allies will gain new heart and spirit in your company. I wish that I could shake the hand of each one of you, and bid you God speed on your mission.

The review of American troops on St George's Plateau, Independence Day, 1918.

After the review, the 3,600 men marched to Wavertree Park where 20 marquees now stood. The Americans received a dinner financed by Liverpool Corporation and catered by Cunard, which produced a menu that would not be out of place on one of its liners. The following day the 358th Infantry Regiment departed for France.

The opulent meal was at odds with the local food situation. On 20 July the Walker Art Gallery with the exception of two imminent exhibitions closed to the public at the request of the Food Control Authority. The gallery became the administrative centre for the distribution of 3 tons of ration books. Housewives had until 21 September to register for their new ration books, which would come into operation on 3 November.

While on the Western Front, in a series of bitterly contested engagements, the Allies reversed German fortunes. On 15 July, near Reims, Ludendorff launched his final great offensive but made little progress. Three days later a Franco-American counter-attack supported by masses of light tanks drove back the Germans. Depleted of reserves and weakened by 50,000 casualties, on 20 July Ludendorff abandoned his Flanders offensive and went on the defensive. Allied counter-attacks were many, but the most significant of the final blows occurred near Amiens on 8 August. The surprise Anglo-French attack broke against a demoralised enemy increasingly fighting without conviction. General Ludendorff later said '8 August was the black day of the German army in the history of the war . . . it put the decline of our fighting power beyond all doubt'. The Allied advance to victory had begun. The German tide began to ebb and gradually withdrew in the direction of the Fatherland. Ludendorff admitted the war could not be won, but wished to maintain a strong military position to negotiate favourable terms in the inevitable peace treaty, ideally retaining possession of Belgium and Luxembourg. Austria promised to send reinforcements to France, but a few weeks later attempted to broker a peace deal with the United States; it was declined. On 27 September Bulgaria also sought an armistice, followed by the abdication of their monarch.

The final blows inflicted heavy casualties on the inexperienced American troops whose seriously wounded filtered through to Liverpool. By late September, only two wards required completion at Mossley Hill which now had nine wards for bed cases, including one for officers, a surgical ward, nine barrack huts, a large recreation hut,

The kitchen at Mossley Hill Red Cross Hospital.

a kitchen building and a large dining hall. Mossley House itself was used for administration and nurses' sleeping quarters. In the event of an emergency a further 300 patients could be cared for in fully equipped tents. Tending the patients were 18 officers, 60 nurses and 150 enlisted men.

The Americans also benefitted from a scheme initiated by the Liverpool branch of the Rotary Club, itself of American origin, which was taken up across the nation. Wounded American soldiers on the last week of their convalescence, which was the only opportunity army regulations allowed, were entertained as honoured guests in private homes. Where they would 'learn at first hand the nature of our home life, so that in writing home, and when they return home as living epistles, they may clear the air of the poison mists, which our enemies, with their usual thoroughness, are spreading over there in the hope of weakening the alliance which we believe is to prove fatal to their hopes'. The scheme was evidently a great success as during the twelve months of its existence, four different Commanding Officers of Mossley Hill Military Hospital wrote favourable letters of appreciation.

Another recipient of a letter was the Mayor of Bootle who responded to the request of the commander of HMS *Bootle* (a Hunt class minesweeper) and forwarded a framed picture of the Bootle coat of arms. This gesture paled into insignificance when compared with the £800,000 Bootle raised in War Bonds and certificates and this effort was recognised by two aircraft carrying the name Bootle.

Another airborne threat was the Spanish influenza epidemic, and its emergence in Liverpool during late October led to a precautionary three-week closure of Liverpool schools. Bootle closed schools until 4 November having had twenty influenza deaths in one week. The public were advised to avoid crowded rooms. Nonetheless, during the week ending 30 October, Liverpool recorded 230 flu deaths.

Regardless of the risk to their health, the 27 Red Cross VAD continued to drive the ambulances of the Liverpool BRCS and the Liverpool Civic Service League. In the five weeks ending on 22 October they carried over 6,600 patients (2,000 were American), and more than half were stretcher cases including influenza and septic pneumonia victims. During its existence Belmont Road Military Hospital had 222 deaths, more than half being American soldiers with influenza that landed at Liverpool.

The war was also in terminal decline and in late September the Turkish armies in Palestine were defeated. Faced with the collapse of the alliance between the Central Powers, Germany became increasingly isolated which prompted Ludendorff to demand an armistice, to which the Kaiser agreed. On 5 November the Admiralty announced they had successfully defeated the submarines and maintained a huge convoy system. Of the 85,772 merchant ships convoyed only 433 were lost. Germany's key allies, Turkey and Austria-Hungary, signed armistices on 30 November and 3 November respectively. Germany's own peace negotiations stalled over President Wilson's insistence on the abdication of Kaiser Wilhelm II. Exasperated by the Kaiser's reluctance, the German Chancellor forced the hand of Wilhelm by announcing his abdication on 9 November (he officially abdicated on

28 November). Two days later Germany signed an armistice and suddenly the war ended.

In Liverpool uncertainty over the timing of the ceasefire prevented elaborate preparations. Instead, the new Lord Mayor ordered the flags of all the Entente countries to be displayed on the Town Hall balcony. As each flag was placed in position enthusiastic cheering arose from a large crowd in Castle Street. When the Town Hall received official confirmation of the Armistice, the Lord Mayor, the ex-Lord Mayor (Doctor Utting) and other civic leaders ascended to the Town Hall balcony facing Castle Street. They were greeted with deafening and prolonged cheering. The Lord Mayor said, 'It was with very great pleasure that he had received official confirmation of the news that an armistice had been signed at five o'clock that morning; and at eleven o'clock firing had ceased'.

I WON'T HAVE PEACE UNTIL I HEAR FROM YOU!

The breaking news was tempered with fears for safety of loved ones.

The good news spread like wildfire and thousands of people left work with the result that Castle Street, Water Street and Dale Street were filled with ecstatic crowds and not even the jubilations at the relief of Mafeking paralleled the scenes witnessed in the streets of Liverpool and Bootle. The bells of churches rang joyous peals that mingled with the less musical 'Cock a doodle do' of the steam whistles of the locomotive engines and the river craft. Bootle Town Hall clock had not been heard for four years and now it chimed continuously.

In the afternoon Lord Street, Church Street and Bold Street were almost impassable due to the crowds who cheered anything, especially the wounded Tommies and groups of American soldiers. Soldiers arriving home on leave came in for tremendous ovations as they emerged from the station. One mud-stained hero was promptly picked up and carried shoulder high as he waved flags which had been thrust in his hands. At nightfall St George's Plateau attracted masses of people, and here an impromptu patriotic demonstration took place and national songs were sung with great enthusiasm. The rejoicings continued until a late hour, especially in the vicinity of the Town Hall, the front of which was illuminated with tricoloured electric lights. The *Daily Post and Echo* reported:

> Thanks to a relaxation of the restrictions on lighting, the streets remained crowded until midnight, and the hotels and cafes were able to serve light suppers to those who had arranged to signalise the great event indoors. All theatres and halls were crowded, and the performances were punctuated with patriotic interludes which were keenly relished. The front of the Town Hall was gaily illuminated in honour of the occasion, and the brilliance, coming after such a long period of gloom, was very acceptable in itself, and doubly welcome as a symbol of the passage from the darkness of war to the light of peace.

Warfare on the Western Front had ceased but elsewhere the war continued. A military machine and supporting infrastructure assembled in excess of four years would take time to dismantle and for life to return to normal and families and communities to recover from apocalyptic warfare. Men optimistically posted as missing were presumed dead but with no identified remains families usually waited in vain for glad tidings concerning their loved ones.

The military began to demobilise, with priority being given to miners and other occupations so desperately needed at home. This caused great resentment among men who had signed up for a period designated 'duration of war only' and for most it would be early spring before they returned home. The wounded still needed tending, there

'Yer never have anything so I'll give yer summat' relates to the exasperation at post-war rationing.

would be no remarkable peace-time recovery and indeed for decades legions would die from First World War injuries.

Peace would bring many dividends but the downside was the closure of most munitions factories and the consequent unemployment. The North Haymarket shell factory was ordered to discontinue the night shift, and by 26 November approximately 400 women and 150 men were discharged. Further instructions demanded the rapid demobilisation of the factory and each week a number of employees worked their final shift, culminating on 14 December, when the only remaining workers were the men dismantling the factory. During its lifespan the factory manufactured 32,252 tons of shells, and taking into account the shells ready for government inspection prior to despatch over 1 million shells were produced.

The Treaty of Versailles was symbolically signed on the fifth anniversary of the outbreak of war and formally ended the European war. This made little difference to units including the 17/King's Liverpool who were engaged in Northern Russia against the Bolsheviks. It would be early September 1919 before the last of the battalion boarded the troopship for home. Sadly, the uncompromising and humiliating terms of surrender reluctantly accepted by a vanquished Germany produced a festering resentment; two decades later the world would again be at war.

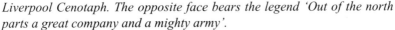

Liverpool Cenotaph. The opposite face bears the legend 'Out of the north parts a great company and a mighty army'.

The Liverpool Cenotaph on St George's Plateau, the work of G. H. Tyson-Smith, has two 80ft-long bronze panels. Prior to the unveiling on 30 November 1930, the cenotaph was covered with a vast pall of sateen, to which 12,000 Flanders poppies had been sewn, and which bore also a huge Union Jack and, in scarlet, the word 'Triumph'. This striking floral veil had been made by lady workers, aided by ex-servicemen. For the unveiling an electric device had been installed requiring Lord Derby only to press a button.

Bootle War Memorial was unveiled on 15 October 1922 by retired former 7/King's commander Major James Burnie MC.

Images of the two Liverpool Pals friezes suspended from the ceiling of Lime Street station. They were unveiled by Prince Edward on 31 August 2014, the 100th anniversary of the raising of the Liverpool Pals. One memorial depicts the enlistment and departure of the pals. The other portrays the pals on the battlefield and their return home.

Bibliography and Further Reading

History and Statistics of the 358th Infantry, 90th Division United States Army, Gerolstein (Germany), 1 May 1919

The Medical Department of the United States Army in the World War, Vol. II, United States Government Printing Office, 1927

Middlebrook, Martin. *The First Day of the Somme*, London, Penguin Books Ltd, 1981

Newspapers and Periodicals.
Birkenhead News
Liverpool Courier
Liverpool Daily Post and Mercury
Liverpool Echo
Liverpool Evening Express
War Illustrated

Index